Out of the Ordinary

Finding Hidden Threats by Analyzing Unusual Behavior

JOHN HOLLYWOOD, DIANE SNYDER,
KENNETH McKAY, JOHN BOON

Approved for public release, distribution unlimited

This research in the public interest was supported by RAND, using discretionary funds made possible by the generosity of RAND's donors, the fees earned on client-funded research, and independent research and development (IR&D) funds provided by the Department of Defense.

Library of Congress Cataloging-in-Publication Data

Out of the ordinary : finding hidden threats by analyzing unusual behavior / John Hollywood ... [et al.].
    p. cm.
    "MG-126."
    Includes bibliographical references.
    ISBN 0-8330-3520-7 (pbk. : alk. paper)
      1. Criminal behavior, Prediction of—United States. 2. Crime forecasting—United States. 3. Criminal methods—United States. 4. Terrorism—Forecasting. 5. Terrorism—Psychological aspects. 6. Intelligence service—United States. 7. National security—United States. I. Hollywood, John S., 1973– II. Rand Corporation.

HV6080.O97 2004
363.32—dc22

2003023703

Cover photograph by Kenneth N. McKay. The photograph is of the "Warabe-Jizo" statue in the Yusei-in Garden of the Sanzen-in Temple in Ohara, Japan. The statue is of a child bodhisattva-kshitigarbha. He is a figure from both the Hindu and Buddhist religions. Derived from the Mother Earth, he appeared in the world to help people.

The RAND Corporation is a nonprofit research organization providing objective analysis and effective solutions that address the challenges facing the public and private sectors around the world. RAND's publications do not necessarily reflect the opinions of its research clients and sponsors.

RAND® is a registered trademark.

Published 2004 by the RAND Corporation
1700 Main Street, P.O. Box 2138, Santa Monica, CA 90407-2138
1200 South Hayes Street, Arlington, VA 22202-5050
201 North Craig Street, Suite 202, Pittsburgh, PA 15213-1516
RAND URL: http://www.rand.org/
To order RAND documents or to obtain additional information, contact
Distribution Services: Telephone: (310) 451-7002;
Fax: (310) 451-6915; Email: order@rand.org

Preface

This monograph presents a unique approach to "connecting the dots" in intelligence—selecting and assembling disparate pieces of information to produce a general understanding of a threat. Modeled after key thought processes used by successful and proactive problem solvers to identify potential threats, the schema described in this document identifies out-of-the-ordinary, atypical behavior that is potentially related to terror activity; seeks to understand the behavior by putting it into context; generates and tests hypotheses about what the atypical behavior might mean; and prioritizes the results, focusing analysts' attention on the most significant atypical findings. In addition to discussing the schema, this document describes a supporting conceptual architecture that dynamically tailors the analysis in response to discoveries about the observed behavior and presents specific techniques for identifying and analyzing out-of-the-ordinary information.

We believe the monograph would be of greatest interest to people in the homeland security community who are interested in connecting the dots across disparate analysis groups and databases to detect and prevent terror attacks. However, it should also interest anyone who needs to monitor large and disparate data streams looking for uncertain and unclear indicators that, taken together, represent potential risks. Thus, we can see the schema and architecture described in this paper having an application in computing security (which involves recognizing indicators of an impending cyber attack) or in public health (which involves recognizing indicators of an impending disease outbreak), for example.

This monograph results from the RAND Corporation's continuing program of self-sponsored independent research. Support for such research is provided, in part, by donors and by the independent research and development provisions of RAND's contracts for the operation of its U.S. Department of Defense federally funded research and development centers. This research was overseen by the RAND National Security Research Division (NSRD). NSRD conducts research and analysis for the Office of the Secretary of Defense, the Joint Staff, the Unified Commands, the defense agencies, the Department of the Navy, the U.S. intelligence community, allied foreign governments, and foundations.

The RAND Corporation Quality Assurance Process

Peer review is an integral part of all RAND research projects. Prior to publication, this document, as with all documents in the RAND monograph series, was subject to a quality assurance process to ensure that the research meets several standards, including the following: The problem is well formulated; the research approach is well designed and well executed; the data and assumptions are sound; the findings are useful and advance knowledge; the implications and recommendations follow logically from the findings and are explained thoroughly; the documentation is accurate, understandable, cogent, and temperate in tone; the research demonstrates understanding of related previous studies; and the research is relevant, objective, independent, and balanced. Peer review is conducted by research professionals who were not members of the project team.

RAND routinely reviews and refines its quality assurance process and also conducts periodic external and internal reviews of the quality of its body of work. For additional details regarding the RAND quality assurance process, visit http://www.rand.org/standards/.

Contents

CHAPTER THREE

The Atypical Signal Analysis and Processing Architecture 35

CHAPTER FOUR

Finding the Dots 65

Figures

Tables

Summary

The problem of "connecting the dots" in intelligence—selecting and assembling disparate pieces of information to produce a general understanding of a threat—has been given great priority since the September 11, 2001, terrorist attacks.[1] This monograph summarizes a RAND internal research and development project on developing unique approaches to assist in connecting the dots.

Synthesizing disparate pieces of information to understand threats is an extremely difficult challenge. The analysis process requires searching through enormous volumes of data, and analysts' attention must be directed to the most important findings. There are, however, few direct clues as to which data are important and how to link the data together. The most obvious approach to prioritizing data—looking for patterns similar to those of previous attacks—can easily lead to missing the signals indicating the next, different attack. When analyzing uncertain and messy (i.e., real-world) data, time and situational pressures often force the analyst into making conclusions, despite great uncertainty as to whether the conclusions are true. Ex-

---

[1] As one example of the high priority placed on this topic, the Congressional Joint Inquiry into September 11 writes, in its "Conclusion—Factual Findings" section: "No one will ever know what might have happened had more connections been drawn between these disparate pieces of information. We will never definitively know to what extent the Community would have been able and willing to exploit fully all the opportunities that may have emerged. The important point is that the Intelligence Community, for a variety of reasons, did not bring together and fully appreciate a range of information that could have greatly enhanced its chances of uncovering and preventing Usama Bin Laden's plan to attack these United States on September 11th, 2001."

isting legal, technological, procedural, and cultural barriers to sharing and linking information further complicate these challenges.

A Schema for Connecting the Dots

Historically, however, many people have surmounted the barriers to connecting the dots, albeit with significantly smaller amounts of data than the homeland security community faces. These successful problem solvers have tended to follow similar cognitive processes. First, the problem solver establishes expectations for what the environment will be like if everything is "normal"—in effect, defining a *status quo*. This formulation is employed because it is often impossible to predict everything that is abnormal; instead, it is much easier to describe the status quo as the starting point and add to this description what is known about how the status quo might change. The problem solver next identifies a set of metrics (both quantitative and qualitative) with which to observe the environment, especially in regard to whether the actual environment is consistent with expectations. Third, the problem solver observes streams of measurement data about the environment. Generally, the solver does not examine every observation carefully but instead scans for *out-of-the-ordinary* or *atypical* signals that significantly deviate from the expected status quo. These signals range from defined precursors of a well-understood change in the environment to an entirely novel phenomenon whose meaning is unknown—except that it is in some way relevant to the task at hand.[2] All, however, deserve additional analysis: Because they are outside of expectations for what the current environment should exhibit, they

---

[2] It is important to reiterate that the problem solver does not try to examine all atypical behavior in the environment; doing so would lead to data overload. Instead, the solver pays attention to relevant behavior that can quickly be related to the task at hand. For example, suppose the problem solver is responsible for identifying potential threats to a theme park. Clearly, many attendees in the theme park will engage in "unusual" behavior. The problem solver, however, will be interested strictly in behavior that can quickly be declared potentially relevant to attacks on the theme park, such as a group of guests on a terror watch list, or a group of guests who engage in behavior that strikes the park's security guards as threatening (casing behavior, clandestine communications, etc.).

may signal an impending change in the environment. Upon discovering out-of-the-ordinary behavior, the solver looks for supporting data marking the observed signals as a true phenomenon and not just noise. Should such supporting data be discovered, the problem solver searches for related information that helps explain the phenomenon and then develops and tests hypotheses as to what the phenomenon means. Finally, once the phenomenon is understood, and identified as indicating a risk, the problem solver uses heuristics to avoid or mitigate the risk. It should be noted that the process the problem solver uses is not linear—the solver separates the noise from the truly significant through an iterative, multistage process of testing and learning, with the steps used being dependent on what the solver learns about the phenomenon at each stage (i.e., *context-dependent* analysis).

We have developed the **Atypical Signal Analysis and Processing** (ASAP) schema to assist in connecting the dots by mirroring the problem-solving process described above. An implementation of the schema will serve as an analyst's "virtual extension," applying the problem-solving process to the volumes of data and numbers of dimensions within the data that are far too large for analysts to work with directly. Figure S.1 shows the schema.

The shortest, linear path through the schema has six major steps. The schema begins with the gathering of information from a set of external databases. Most of the information pertains to *watched entities*—people, places, things, and financial activities already suspected as being relevant to a terror attack or activities within key infrastructure and commercial processes already being monitored, such as international commerce, nuclear energy, hazardous materials, and air transportation. Intelligence and government databases would be used, supplemented by open-source data, all in accordance with privacy regulations. This baseline information would be further supplemented by *precedent-setting phenomena*—data, voluntarily submitted, that describes behavior the reporters find to be highly out of the ordinary and suspicious with respect to asymmetric threats. (For ex-

Figure S.1
The Atypical Signal Analysis and Processing (ASAP) Schema

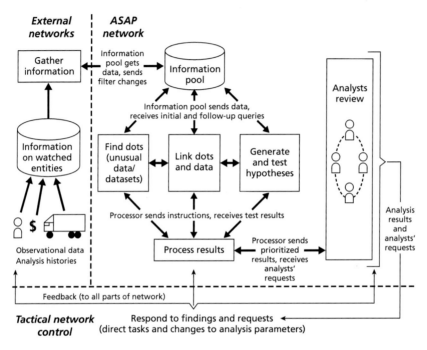

RAND*MG126-S.1*

ample, prior to the 9/11 attacks, FBI officials might have submitted their suspicions about certain flight school students.) The schema incorporates both direct observations of the watched entities and metadata on who is working with those observations and why. The resulting information goes into a structured information pool.

Second, within the pool, a number of automated detection agents perpetually filter the information to look for out-of-the-ordinary signals.[3] These signals might be single observations (e.g., a

---

[3] Note that an ASAP network would not detect and process all atypical signals; instead, it would process atypical signals that can be quickly classified as being potentially relevant to an attack or the operations of a terrorist organization. For the former, a network would seek atypical signals potentially related to attack preparations such as target casing, training, clandestine communications, supply (smuggling), and weapons acquisition. For example, from a theme park, the network would be interested in hearing reports of people videotaping secu-

very large financial transfer) or a significant trend (e.g., a 75 percent increase in fund transfers during the past month). The signals might also be a group studying information they do not normally review (e.g., an FBI field office requesting records of students at truck driving schools funded by the aforementioned increase in funding transfers). Such signals become the "dots." Note that ASAP will support detection filters ranging in sophistication from simple rules evaluating a few data fields (usually generated by human analysts) to complicated algorithms evaluating tens of simultaneous data fields simultaneously (usually generated by hybrid human-machine statistical training techniques, such as neural networks).

Third, once the dots have been identified, the next step is to find information related to the dots. The schema thus employs automated relationship agents to look for relationships between new and existing dots. It also uses agents to perform *backsweeping*—searching for previously unremarkable data that relate to the dots. These related data would come primarily from the information pool but also from queries in external (intelligence) databases and, in cases constituting probable cause, from commercial databases (for example, examining the credit transactions of a positively identified terror suspect).[4] The information discovered helps determine the extent of an out-of-the-ordinary phenomenon and provides a context to help explain it.

Fourth, once the dots have been linked, hypothesis agents can be tasked to create possible interpretations for the linked dots and to create corresponding testing plans to determine whether the hypotheses are correct. The principal purpose of these agents is to assess which phenomena should be given priority for further investigation.

---

rity checkpoints and support beams of major attractions; it would not be interested in hearing reports on generic disorderly conduct. For the latter, a network would seek atypical signals such as sudden movements, changes in organizational structure, or changes in communications networks. The issue of what constitutes "out of the ordinary" is discussed at length in Chapter Two.

[4] Backsweeping in probable-cause cases is the only time the ASAP schema would use general commercial databases. Thus, for example, the schema complies with the proposed Citizens' Protection in Federal Databases Act, which would prohibit accessing databases "based solely on a hypothetical scenario or hypothetical supposition of who may commit a crime or pose a threat to national security."

Consequently, the "hypotheses" very often do not pertain to a specific inference but instead simply note that a phenomenon is so unusual (and perhaps has particularly suspicious characteristics) that it is worth investigating further. Correspondingly, the testing agents monitor whether further investigations raise or lower concern about the phenomenon.

Fifth, the results of these processes are strictly prioritized, and high-priority results are forwarded to analysts. This prioritization function is one of the most important of the schema, as it reduces potentially large volumes of out-of-the ordinary discoveries, so that analysts can restrict their attention to only the most relevant and significant discoveries.

Finally, the schema facilitates the collaboration of analysts working on related observations. It notifies different analysts that they are looking at the same pieces of information and provides communications channels between them. In the ASAP schema, analysts have primary responsibility for actions to be taken in response to unusual phenomena that are brought to their attention because they have insights (knowledge of human behavior, for instance) that automated systems do not have.

As with human problem solvers, the schema permits iterative, dynamically tailored analysis in which the actual sequences of testing activities are dependent on what has been learned to date about the observed phenomena. To allow for such context-dependent processing, the complete schema is governed by a two-stage control system. At the lower, operational level, processor agents direct data through the schema. These agents use sets of control rules to interpret the results from the detection, relationship, and hypothesis agents, and determine what to do next with a particular dataset (or test results on the dataset). Thus, for example, a processor agent might direct a newly detected dot to a relationship agent and forward results from hypothesis testing to analysts. This structure allows for flows through ASAP to be both dynamic and iterative. Thus, analysis results guide what happens next, so that, for example, analyzing one initial signal leads to the discovery of related phenomena, which are then further analyzed, leading to yet more contextual information, and so on, potentially allowing an initially mysterious phenomenon to be illuminated fully. Processor agents are guided both by automated logic and directions from analysts. Analysts have the ability to request any type of follow-up test or analysis of the ASAP agents, with the processor agents executing these requests.

At the second, tactical level, the ASAP is subject to open-loop control: Analysts may change any of the software agents and agents' parameters, or make any specific analysis requests, in response to the analysis results. The tactical level also supports automated control agents that modify software agents and parameters based on interpretation of finding, relating, and testing dots (these software control agents are also subject to analysts' direction).

We have developed an architectural design that applies the schema; description of the design makes up the bulk of this paper. The design has several key attributes worth mentioning here.

First, in its initial stages the architecture focuses on information already suspected of being of interest, as opposed to performing unguided data mining of large databases and collecting data about generic transactions. This focus helps prevent analytic overload. At the same time, the architecture has the flexibility both to receive reports of highly atypical behavior from all sources and to cull databases for particular pieces of information should the need arise (for example, searching for data about a highly suspicious person's travel plans).

Second, the architecture searches primarily for signals that are out of the ordinary as opposed to signals that fit predetermined patterns. This approach loses precision in meaning but gains in being able to detect a wide range of threatening behavior that does not fit previously seen attack patterns. Searching for signals deviating from, rather than matching, existing patterns is uncommon in the pattern-matching and signal analysis fields.

Third, in finding dots, searching for related information, and generating hypotheses, the architecture employs contextual rules that allow data to be analyzed in the context of existing knowledge. Contextual rules are not commonly used in information analysis.

Fourth, the architecture explicitly deals with uncertainty by generating and testing competing hypotheses for unusual signals. This approach helps defend against prematurely accepting an explanation for a phenomenon.

Finally, the architecture enables the collaboration of personnel needed to connect the dots, even if the personnel are distributed across different groups and agencies. The architecture looks not just for out-of-the-ordinary data, but for *out-of-the-ordinary analyses of the data*. Flagging these analyses can bring together groups of people and automated agents who can jointly characterize a previously mysterious phenomenon.

Near-Term Implementation

Fully implementing the ASAP schema and its supporting architecture would be a lengthy, multiyear process. However, several improvements could be implemented quickly, in effect allowing personal analysis interactions to partially substitute for the automated agents described previously.

A major requirement for detecting out-of-the-ordinary phenomena is to understand what constitutes "ordinary" and what types of behaviors are significant deviations away from the ordinary that may be relevant to a counterterrorism investigation. Thus, we recommend that appropriate users throughout the homeland security (HLS) community create and distribute standardized profiles of organized behavior. These profiles would discuss both what threats (terror attacks, terror support activities, etc.) commonly look like and what status-quo conditions look like in such "watched" fields as international commerce, transportation, and demolition. Note that these brief profiles are in no way intended to be comprehensive; their purpose is merely to help analysts and field professionals in one area educate analysts and field professionals in other areas—in a more intentional and systematic way than at present—on what types of behavior to look out for.

The next step would be to establish electronic posting boards where those in the field can report unusual phenomena and see whether others have been observing similar or related occurrences—in effect, helping each other serve as detection and linking agents. Personnel would post to unmoderated electronic bulletin boards, and there would be no approval process for phenomena posted. Trained reviewers would routinely review the boards, selecting especially unusual and significant reports to post to filtered boards that would be widely read by analysts.

The third step would be to develop semiautomated tools to help HLS personnel identify posts relevant to what they have been observing. One might first implement organizational tools that divide the posts into threads dedicated to particular occurrences and create indices of those threads. Particularly important threads would be associated with journals or diaries summarizing key developments and current hypotheses. The next step would to be create Google-like search engines for posts that match the results of search queries. Finally, simple heuristics could be developed that look for connections and patterns across the threads of posted messages.

Summarizing the Schema

Table S.1 summarizes differences between the proposed schema and traditional methods of intelligence analysis. The table also compares a near-term, manual implementation of ASAP with a full implementation.

A Research Plan

At the same time as the short-term improvements are being implemented, research can begin on the automated portions of the ASAP architecture. This portion will be needed to assist analysts in identifying out-of-the-ordinary signals in the enormous volume of data generated by intelligence and infrastructure collection and monitoring systems every day.

Table S.1
The ASAP Schema

Traditional Analysis	ASAP Advantages	ASAP Near-Term Implementation	Full ASAP System Implementation
Focuses on previous patterns	Searches for out-of-the-ordinary behavior, allowing for detection of previously unseen threats	Core or pilot group	New communities added to electronic boards
Time pressure drives toward premature closure	Allows memory of hypotheses and data rejected by analysts	Drafting short profiles of existing asymmetric threats—e.g., suicide bombing	Incorporates entire homeland security community
Analysts mostly operate on basis of own experience and biases	Leaves key analytic choices with analysts	Drafting short profiles of status quo in such watched domains as international commerce	Detailed architecture for out-of-the-ordinary analysis
Search tools mostly weed out what doesn't fit pattern	Notices what analysts are watching and asking	Users post on unmoderated electronic boards	Formal specifications for detection, linking, and hypothesis agents
Analysts are isolated within own groups and agencies	Facilitates collaboration between analysts studying the same phenomena	Moderators connect across analysts and, when possible, organizations	Analysis processes integrated across organizations

The first stage of research should develop a detailed architectural plan for the ASAP system and its constituent control and analysis agents. The architecture would specifically describe detection, linking, and hypothesis agents in such key areas as direct threat detection, international shipping, and air transportation. The first stage should also describe how the architecture would address a detailed terror-attack scenario.

The second stage of research should create formal design specifications for the agents and the software making up the ASAP backbone. These specifications would define the objects, methods, and major algorithms employed by the agents and systems management software.

The third stage of research should create a prototype system that would include simple examples of the above agents. It would also include the control components needed to achieve dynamic, feedback-based control. Once the prototype is completed and evaluated, construction and implementation of a real-world ASAP system could commence, moving the ASAP concept from research to reality.

Acknowledgments

First and foremost, we thank the RAND Independent Research and Development group for generously funding and supporting this research. The group includes James Thomson, Michael Rich, Brent Bradley, Rachel Swanger, and C. Richard Neu. We also thank Jeff Isaacson and Kevin O'Connell for their support of this project on behalf of the National Security Research Division. We especially want to thank Kevin O'Connell for his personal support of this project, as well as for his very useful insights on ways to improve the research. In addition, we thank Greg Treverton, Robert Anderson, and William Mularie for their reviews of this monograph and for their useful recommendations. We also thank RAND colleagues John Parachini, Paul Davis, Martin Libicki, and Shari Pfleeger for meeting with us and providing the research group with important insights.

Acronyms

AHEAD	Analogical Hypothesis Elaborator for Activity Detection
ARDA	Advanced Research and Development Activity
ARG	alternate reality game
ASAP	Atypical Signal Analysis and Processing
CIA	Central Intelligence Agency
CT	counterterrorism
CTC	Counter Terrorism Center (Central Intelligence Agency)
DARPA	Defense Advanced Research Projects Agency
DEA	Drug Enforcement Agency
DEFT	Data Extraction From Text
DI	Directorate of Intelligence (Central Intelligence Agency)
DHS	Department of Homeland Security
DO	Directorate of Operations (Central Intelligence Agency)
EWR	early warning and response
FBI	Federal Bureau of Investigation
GISI	Gateway Information Sharing Initiative
HAZMAT	hazardous materials

HLS	homeland security
IC	intelligence community
INS	Immigration and Naturalization Service
INR	Intelligence and Research (U.S. State Department)
NIMD	Novel Intelligence from Massive Data
NORA	Non-Obvious Relationship Awareness
NSA	National Security Agency
SEAS	Structured Evidential Argumentation System
SIAM	Situational Influence Assessment Model
SIGINT	signals intelligence
TIA	Terrorism Information Awareness
XML	extensible markup language

CHAPTER ONE

Introduction

> "I think anything out of the ordinary routine of life well worth reporting."
>
> Sherlock Holmes, in Sir Arthur Conan Doyle's
> *The Hound of the Baskervilles*

Prologue: Something Bad Happened on November 9th

(A hypothetical but unfortunately realistic case study)

In conducting a post-mortem of the sad events of November 9th, it is important to consider the events and timelines leading up to the incident. By mid-November, the media were clamoring for details on who knew what, what was known when, how the "obvious" signals could have been missed, and how the "dots" could have failed to have been "connected" . . . again. By the middle of December, investigative reporters and official government investigators had disclosed that the following observations had existed in various government databases (federal and local) since the middle of October:

February 4
- Two dozen tuna boats are ordered in Seattle for export to Singapore under Panamanian ownership.

June 13
- A city permit is issued for an Arab student forum to be held in Hong Kong in mid-November.

August 9
- Two dozen new tuna boats eventually arrive and register in Sydney's harbor.

September 8
- A Panamanian-registered company makes an application for eighteen berths for tuna boats in Singapore.

October 2
- At a reception at the British Embassy in Singapore, an Australian diplomat reports hiring and work oddities in Sydney harbor involving new tuna boats being repainted.

October 4
- In Singapore, a new firm registered in Panama is reported as trying to pressure local officials to approve special berthing privileges on very short notice without the proper paperwork.

October 6–7
- Over a hundred Arab students from ten countries book travel for November 10 to Hong Kong through Singapore.

October 10
- A wharf in Philadelphia is leased to a Panamanian firm.

October 11
- A routine inspection at a wharf in Philadelphia identifies what appear to be tuna boats off-loading heavy crates.

October 12
- Two Arab students are detained for having false driver licenses in Singapore.
- Abandoned luggage is found at the Singapore airport and a report is filed.

As the investigation continued, a few points became clear. The first was that although some of the above data points (the "dots") were clearly suspicious in retrospect, it would have been virtually impossible to pick them out of the huge volume of noise inherent in modern intelligence processing and analysis, even with standard filtering techniques. Similarly, although the connections between the dots were also obvious in retrospect, the intelligence community and homeland security agencies simply were not designed to support the discovery of such links or to perform the follow-on analysis needed to determine what the connected dots might mean. New strategies were clearly needed. . . .

(Appendix A presents the complete case study of the "November 9th affair.")

The Problem of Connecting the Dots in Intelligence

Too small. Too few. Too sparse. Too irregular. Too contextual. These characteristics of data about the "bad guys" are today's challenges. Predicting how adversaries will act is easy to do in hindsight but hard to do in advance. If their behavior is regular, or if the challenge is bounded, analyses that identify systematic behavior can be and have been successful. However, with the current and growing asymmetric threats, new tools are needed to exploit characteristics that are too small, too few, too sparse, too irregular, and too contextual.

Traditional approaches have assumed larger, more observable, less agile, and less creative adversaries. The new adversaries are far less tangible and more elusive. The challenge is compounded by a growing data glut, increasing noise in the environment and decreasing time available to perform analysis. To complicate matters, we cannot assume that the adversary will attack the same way twice. Projects such as the Novel Intelligence from Massive Data (NIMD) program[1] propose innovative ways to deal with some of these challenges and have significant potential to help find entirely new and meaningful relationships in large-scale data sources. However, a key aspect not addressed by the projects of which the authors are aware is how analysts initially identify points of interest that do not meet narrowly de-

---

[1] NIMD is sponsored by the Advanced Research and Development Activity (ARDA). For more information, see http://www.ic-arda.org/Novel_Intelligence/.

fined criteria—in other words, the dots. The closest analogy to this key part of the process is that of astute problem solvers who, like the fictional Sherlock Holmes, track certain characteristics to recognize *out-of-the-ordinary* situations that can yield clues about events and activities. *Something was supposed to be there but was not. Something was there but it wasn't supposed to be. The activities are unusual—our suspects are acting differently.* These out-of-the-ordinary observations yield insights into what may happen in the future.

Another key aspect not commonly addressed is how to connect the dots—to identify the context of the out-of-the-ordinary data and to generate and test hypotheses related to what the connected dots might mean. In the past, when the amount of available intelligence information was comparatively limited, analysts could keep track of a complete picture of a situation. For example, R. V. Jones (1978) explicitly notes how having one analyst accessing the complete information stream and seeing the big picture was critical for many World War II intelligence successes. However, in World War II, comparatively all-seeing analysts were possible since data gathering was largely manual and limited by scarce resources. The challenge today is much greater, given both the volumes of intelligence information available and the numerous technical, organizational, and policy barriers to synthesizing information from multiple sources.

The intelligence community (IC) today draws on a disparate, heterogeneous assortment of collection and analysis systems, many of which were designed without any intention that their inputs and outputs would ever be used in an integrated, cooperative fashion. Since the mid-1980s, the IC has focused on developing numerous analysis support systems, knowing that it will need to draw on data in every imaginable form. However, we are not even to the point of having all necessary data in electronic form. Historically, both technical and nontechnical barriers—such as organizational policies, cultures, and security—have limited the usefulness of analytic support tools. Nonetheless, recent progress in integrating collection and automated analysis systems and in organizational collaboration through task forces, interagency centers, and ad-hoc working groups has increased the prospect for dramatic improvements in data analysis.

To date, most analytical support tools have leveraged what the tools' designers thought the technology could provide, coupled with their perceptions of analysts' needs. Sadly, some systems were designed and delivered without close consultation with the end-user. Another consistent problem is that collection and analytical systems have been designed and applied using conventional mindsets and approaches. Research in how analysts do their work has repeatedly shown that analysts become prisoners of their own experience, biases, and cognitive limitations (Heuer, 1999). Many analysts designed their strategy by looking for patterns related to "fighting the last war," and the IC went on building software systems to accommodate analysts doing just that. Other systems were designed to lighten the load on the analyst, to shovel away 90 percent of the low-grade rock so the remaining 10 percent had the highest likelihood of containing the rich ore that the analyst could profitably mine—but the "ore" was defined as information consistent with established patterns. Similarly, those who collected data were led to look specifically for the data analysts believed would fill the missing piece of an established or predicted pattern. Thinking "outside the box" is not a natural behavior for intelligence analysts—or for the human brain. Nonetheless, as Jones and others note, certain analysts have been very successful at doing just that.

In this monograph, we describe a concept for an analysis tool that is based on how the most-effective human analysts think "outside the box" to detect threats—a tool that models how those experts watch for and track the out-of-the-ordinary situations that yield critical insights into an intelligence problem. The analysts' experience and cognitive skills, combined with their intuition, allow them to generate expectations about what they are watching. However, the current human threat detection process suffers from an immense data load, disparate information flows, and time pressures. The proposed tool will complement existing projects, such as NIMD, that augment the human analytic process. Using contextual models created by expert analysts (including machine "analysts"), which describe both "normal" and "significantly atypical" expectations for what is watched and tracked, the tool can detect and track unusual and out-of-the-ordinary situations as they develop.

We propose a multitiered analysis and filtering system to assist analysts: It would monitor *what is watched* over time, *how they are watched*, and *the results of the watching*. What might start out as unusual and mildly out of the ordinary may change in perspective as other out-of-the-ordinary observations are clustered and analyzed for interdependencies of such factors as time, geography, and finances. The results can focus, guide, and concentrate specific and detailed information searches and analyses that use other analytical tools available or under development.

When the proposed detector is coupled with tools for processing structures and correlating data and activities, an integrated preemptive analysis system results. The **Atypical Signal Analysis and Processing** (ASAP) **system** addresses the asymmetric threat from all information fronts—what is out there, what is developing and gaining momentum, and what other players are involved. We believe that ASAP would be an important tool for warning the United States of developing and impending asymmetric threats.

Cognitive Processes for Connecting the Dots

McKay has carried out an extended research agenda over the past 15 years on problem solvers in dynamic situations.[2] This research has yielded insights into how humans proactively identify potential risks and their likely consequences; its results are the inspiration for the ASAP system.

McKay shows that proactive problem solvers monitor populations and key data streams, pick up the extraordinary signals that could indicate a potential risk, and then initiate additional information analyses as needed to illuminate the risk. Note that "could indi-

---

[2] Described, for example, in McKay and Wiers (2003); McKay, Safayeni, and Buzacott (1995a); McKay (1992); and McKay, Buzacott, Charness, and Safayeni (1992).

cate a potential risk" is an important distinction; the problem solver does not analyze all instances of atypical behavior but only those observations that can quickly be declared "potentially relevant" to a particular risk. Heuristics are then used to reduce or avoid the anticipated problem. The study subjects watched both people and processes and used intuitive models of the watched to pick out behaviors and characteristics that were odd, unusual, or threatening. Their mental models were based on expected behaviors—actions and activities. Behaviors were watched over time and changes were tracked. Sudden changes, a series of changes, frequent changes, a high magnitude of change, and changes that fit into potentially threatening contexts all warranted raised eyebrows. If the situation was sufficiently different from what it had been in the past, it was examined more closely. If the situation was assessed to be potentially important, the immediate or short-term past was *backswept* to detect initially ignored signals that might be relevant to the situation. The analysts were also aware of *clustering;* if they made an increasing number of odd or interesting observations, their level of alertness and analysis rose significantly. The analysts would also look to see what was related to the unusual events, what the correlation was, and whether events were converging. Expert problem solvers, who have the job of foreseeing future difficulties and discounting them, go through this process continually—often without conscious effort. To them, it is second nature to recognize the dots and connect them. The initial trigger is usually a change in the status quo.

Studied in isolation, a single or minor change might not be noteworthy, but when placed in context of what has happened in the past and what else might be happening simultaneously, the change suddenly becomes important. Experts have been observed exhibiting this type of behavior in a routine and subconscious fashion. For example, consider an observation from McKay's six-month study of one individual. The planner in a large factory being studied had an idea of normal email traffic between two of the factory's organizations that he was watching. Over two weeks, the amount of email traffic slowly increased. When it had increased to a level beyond what was considered normal, the planner noted that the status quo had changed and that certain events might happen in the future. He anticipated that a meeting would take place on a specific date and involve certain individuals, notably including factory managers. As a result, he specifically planned critical manufacturing events to take place before and after the anticipated meeting—when the managers would be available for supervision and support. Figure 1.1 summarizes this example.

The planner was right in his prediction of the meeting. Further, during the research study, the planner detected over 75 percent of the major perturbations to the factory and made appropriate corrections 60 to 80 percent of the time—an impressive score.

As another example, intelligence analysts have been observed to have an expectation about how certain materiel assets will be configured and deployed. A movement of the assets to a different region—out of the normal area of operation—could indicate that something unusual is going on. The movements of German radar groups were monitored in this way during World War II when intelligence was being sought for the test site of the V-2 rocket (described in Jones, 1978). The email traffic and materiel examples are the types of early warning indicators that lead to proactive intervention. These examples are not particularly unusual and have been observed in a number of cognitive studies of problem solvers. They have also been commented upon by such experts as R. V. Jones and Allen Dulles in their descriptions of the cat-and-mouse activities in scientific and operational intelligence during World War II (Jones, 1978; Dulles, 1963).

The key is to watch, to have expectations about what is being watched, to identify out-of-the-ordinary happenings, and to be able to correlate them with other interesting observations. Those findings are then used to guide further analyses or actions. For example, consider unusual cash transactions combined with unusual travel patterns of members of an extremist party during a period just prior to the anniversary of a suicide bombing. They might not mean anything, but they are worth a second look.

It is important to note that the problem-solving processes described above are much less linear than they appear at first glance. A

Figure 1.1
How Proactive Problem Solvers Connect the Dots

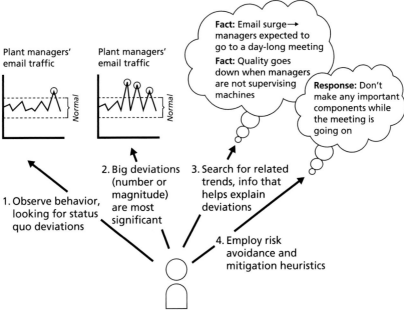

SOURCE: Ethnographic research by K. N. McKay.
RAND*MG126-1.1*

problem solver will go through multiple iterations of finding out-of-the-ordinary phenomena, attempting to link them with other information, and generating and testing hypotheses about meaning, with each step based on what the problem solver has learned to date. We call the ability to perform multiple steps in a nonlinear order, with the next determined by what has been learned to date along with other environmental factors, *context-dependent analysis*.

So far, we have examined models and concepts of how skilled, individual analysts watch, collect dots, and subsequently connect them. The models and concepts appear to be commonsense and obvious at one level, but how they actually work and function together is really rather sophisticated. They involve multiple levels of detection, models of status-quo behavior, backsweeping (searching for previously unnoticed data), and connecting possibly related facts. The aggregate model is complicated but works fine when the problem is suitable for an individual to handle. It is possible to train certain people to develop models of the status quo, pick out the unusual as time proceeds, and bring any unexpected changes to the attention of others. In one study (McKay, Buzacott, and Safayeni, 1995b), a junior analyst was trained to recognize the normal from the abnormal—making routine decisions about the normal and seeking help for the remainder. The junior analyst was reportedly able to deal with 80 percent of the decisions in this way. This was a conscious strategy on the part of the senior analyst and allowed him to concentrate on the unusual and nonroutine. Clearly, this type of proactive thinking and problem resolution is a mindset and a cognitive skill shared by good puzzle solvers, game players, planners, and schedulers. For example, good factory planners analyze the situation, identify and connect the key dots, and plan accordingly to minimize the risks of not meeting production quotas or causing quality problems. They anticipate where slack resources should be intelligently placed and plan for needed contingencies.

In small and constrained situations, a human analyst can keep track of watched entities and their associated condition. He can have a sufficiently full picture of those entities' present condition. He can remember their past condition and predict their expected behaviors when necessary. In the field research conducted in the past decade, the problem solving that used proactive detection successfully was narrow, focused, and funneled through a single analyst.

Unfortunately, the single human analyst model does not work for today's intelligence problem. It worked well in World War II's limited collection environment, as noted earlier, and it often works well in factory management. It does not work when the information stream is large, distributed through different agencies or individuals, or when the intelligence problem is so complex that no single person can possibly understand all its nuances.

The challenge is to create assistance tools to help large-scale intelligence processes function like a single brain or entity. The total system needs to be able to detect the unusual and connect the dots as the first order of business just as an expert analyst does. Does it make sense to consider an automated or hybrid detection aid for the intelligence process? That depends. If one is not watching, not collecting, and not speculating about what people are doing, the answer is no. One needs information in the stream, models of expected behavior, and models of relationships on which to apply the aid. However, it does make sense if one is watching and has some knowledge about the status quo or normal behaviors of the watched. We believe the latter is the case—the information about the status quo is "out there"—waiting to be gathered.

The enemy, too, is out there—leaving information traces that describe his behavior. In general, people need shelter, sustenance, transportation, communication, material items, and currency. When viewed in context, these behaviors can yield critical information. Note that we are not saying that everyone in society is worthy of such surveillance and monitoring. This would be impossible to do and would likely yield few new insights. Rather, perceived and potential enemies are already being monitored and watched. Further, enemies who are not being watched frequently engage in highly atypical behavior as part of their attack preparations; these behaviors stand out from the status-quo noise, leading to those enemies being watched as well. This is the population of interest. We are not talking about detailed or specific data elements and their values. We are talking about meta-patterns, types of data, types of activities, and general behaviors. People, objects, activities, and processes have naturally occurring life cycles that can be exploited. Although it may make sense to mine the data for any statistical relationship between details, the power of deduction and detection resides at the higher level. For example, it does not matter what type of military vehicle is seen in a demilitarized zone—any military vehicle would be odd. In a more recent example (the "Beltway Sniper" shootings), it did not matter if a white cube van with ladder racks was detected across distributed road blocks set up in response to nearby shootings; it did matter if any vehicle was detected at multiple road blocks close to the scenes of the crimes.

The intelligence community collects a great deal of data on watched entities and observes and documents many behaviors. Some of the behaviors are routine, but some may indicate a change in operational status or the initiation of a threat. How do we detect the threatening behavior, isolate it from the glut of information, and bring it to the attention of intelligence analysts in a timely fashion? How do we pick out the clues and make sense of them in large-scale systems? These questions are the crux of the problem of connecting the dots.

A Solution for Connecting the Dots—The Atypical Signal Analysis and Processing Schema

The challenge, therefore, is to employ the expert problem solvers' thought processes in an environment that has too much information and too many dimensions to employ the problem solvers directly. We used the proactive problem solvers' thought processes (discussed above) to create the Atypical Signal Analysis and Processing (ASAP) schema.

Figure 1.2 presents the schema. The shortest, linear path through the schema has six major steps. The schema begins with the collection and storage of information on *watched entities*; these entities are already the subjects of government monitoring or have created signals unusual enough to be detected and submitted for further analysis. As with the factory scheduler and the World War II analysts, the schema examines only certain key information streams. In the realm of asymmetric threat detection, these streams would include the following:

- Intelligence streams on entities likely related to terror organizations or showing some indication of being anomalous and worth further study.
- Regulation-enforcement streams on entities involved with such critical systems as international shipping (customs), hazardous

Figure 1.2
The Atypical Signal Analysis and Processing Schema

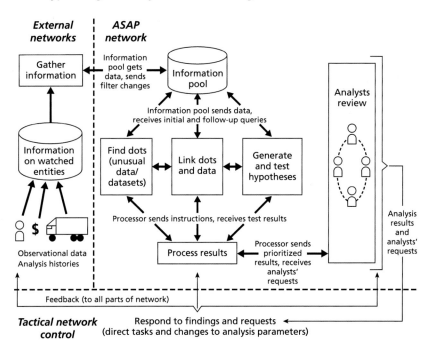

RAND*MG126-1.2*

materials production and transportation, and air transportation. The schema would receive data that either meets some criterion for being anomalous or that meets a specific request for information about particular people or entities; most regulation-enforcement data would not enter an ASAP system

- Voluntary submissions from law-enforcement and security officers, reporting observations they consider to be potentially worth further investigation. Again, the schema would not receive routine law-enforcement or corporate security information except in response to specific, authorized, information requests.[3]

---

[3] Later in this chapter, we discuss near-term recommendations on gaining ASAP-like benefits, including how to work with law enforcement and security officers to collect needed information for ASAP systems.

The ASAP schema is intended to improve analysis of the data the government already collects; it is not seen as a precursor to major collection increases.[4] To help determine what data should be collected, the schema provides a set of interceptor agents that test data in external networks and gather suitable information into an information pool.

Second, from the pool, a series of automated detection agents filters the data, looking for pieces of information sufficiently unusual to be worth further study—the dots. The dots may be detected either because they match some special criteria related to known unusual activities or because they violate criteria related to normal activities. The latter—the detection of truly out-of-the-ordinary information—is of particular interest. This primary detection process is similar to what humans do when they discover information worthy of greater attention (such as when the factory scheduler noticed the surge in email). The ASAP schema can flexibly support detection filters ranging in sophistication from simple rules evaluating a few data fields (usually generated by human analysts) to complicated algorithms evaluating tens of simultaneous data fields simultaneously (usually generated by hybrid human-machine statistical training techniques, such as neural networks).

Once the dots have been identified, the third step is to find information related to them. The schema thus employs agents to look for relationships between new and existing dots. It also uses agents to perform backsweeping—searching for previously unremarkable data that relate to the dots. These related data would come primarily from the information pool but also from queries in external (intelligence) databases and, in cases constituting probable cause, from commercial databases (examining the credit transactions of a positively identified

---

[4] This focus on improving analysis of existing data distinguishes the ASAP schema from other major threat detection proposals, notably DARPA's Terrorism Information Awareness program, which envisions the data mining of massive public databases for terrorism-related patterns (see DARPA's Terrorism Information Awareness web page, http://www.darpa.mil/iao/TIASystems.htm, accessed April 2003).

terror suspect, for instance).[5] The information discovered helps determine the extent of an out-of-the-ordinary phenomenon and provides a context to help explain it.

Once the dots have been linked, the fourth step is to task hypothesis and testing agents to create possible interpretations for the linked dots and to create testing plans to determine whether the hypotheses are correct. The principal purpose of the hypothesis and testing agents is to assess which phenomena should be given priority for further investigation. Consequently, the hypotheses often do not pertain to a specific inference but instead note simply that a phenomenon is so unusual (and perhaps has some characteristics noted as being particularly suspicious) that it is worth investigating further. Correspondingly, the testing agents monitor whether the further investigations raise or lower concern about the phenomena.

Fifth, the results of finding dots, linking them, and generating and testing hypotheses are prioritized, with the most significant results being forwarded to analysts. Prioritization analysis, one of the most important functions of the schema, restricts analysts' attention to the most atypical and significant findings.

Finally, ASAP facilitates the collaboration of analysts working on related observations. It notifies different analysts looking at the same pieces of information and provides communications channels between them. In the ASAP schema, analysts have the primary responsibility for taking actions in response to unusual phenomena that are drawn to their attention, because they have insights (knowledge of human behavior, for instance) that automated systems do not have.

As with human problem solvers, the schema permits iterative, dynamically tailored analysis, in which the actual sequences of activities depend on what has been learned to date about the observed phenomena. To allow for such context-dependent processing, the complete schema is governed by a two-stage control system. At the

---

[5] Backsweeping in probable-cause cases is the only time the ASAP schema would use general commercial databases. Thus, for example, the schema complies with the proposed Citizens' Protection in Federal Databases Act, which would prohibit accessing databases "based solely on a hypothetical scenario or hypothetical supposition of who may commit a crime or pose a threat to national security."

lower, operational level, processor agents direct data through the schema. These agents use sets of control rules to interpret the results from the detection, relationship, and hypothesis agents and determine what to do next with a particular dataset (or test results on the dataset). For example, a processor agent might direct a newly detected dot to a relationship agent and forward results from hypothesis testing to analysts. This structure allows for flows through ASAP to be both dynamic and iterative. Thus, analysis results guide what happens next. For example, analyzing an initial signal may lead to the discovery of related phenomena, which are then further analyzed, leading to yet more contextual information, and so on—potentially allowing an initially mysterious phenomenon to be illuminated fully.

The schema also allows analysts to request any tests or analyses of the ASAP network. The processor agents execute the analysts' requests.

At the second, tactical level, ASAP is subject to open-loop control; analysts may change any of the agents and agents' parameters, or make specific analysis requests, in response to the analysis results. The tactical level also supports automated control agents that modify agents and parameters based on interpreting the results of finding, relating, and testing dots (these control agents are also subject to analysts' control).

Key Attributes of ASAP

We have developed an architectural design that applies the schema; the description of the design comprises the bulk of this paper. The design has several key attributes that set it apart from other computer systems being developed to connect the dots within asymmetric-threat related information. (Appendix B discusses these other systems in detail and how they might complement the ASAP schema or implement some of the schema's components.)

First, the architecture focuses in its initial stages on information already suspected of being of interest, rather than performing unguided data mining of large databases to collect data about generic transactions. This helps prevent analytic overload. This focus on upstream analysis sets ASAP apart from programs like the Defense Advanced Research Projects Agency's (DARPA's) Terrorist Information Awareness (TIA) program, which is intended to operate on very large volumes of generic information (see DARPA Information Awareness Office, 2003c), as well as other intelligence community systems for the initial filtering and processing of very large data streams. We envision an ASAP system's databases containing millions of entities and tens of millions of links, as opposed to the much higher entity and link counts for these other programs. At the same time, the architecture does have the flexibility both to receive reports of highly atypical behavior from all sources and to cull databases for particular pieces of information should the need arise (for example, searching for data about a highly suspicious person's travel plans).

Second, the architecture searches primarily for out-of-the-ordinary signals as opposed to signals fitting predetermined patterns. This makes ASAP fundamentally complementary to programs like TIA's Evidence Extraction and Link Discovery (EELD) program (see DARPA Information Awareness Office, 2003a), the In-Q-Tel-sponsored Non-Obvious Relationship Awareness (NORA) program (see Systems Research and Development, 2002), and other programs described in Appendix B, which focus on matching data to patterns that signify specific illicit activities. ASAP's approach loses precision in meaning but gains in being able to detect a wide range of threatening behavior that does not fit previously seen attack patterns. Searching for signals deviating from, rather than matching, existing patterns is uncommon in the pattern matching and signal analysis fields.

Third, in finding dots, searching for related information, and generating hypotheses, the architecture employs rules that allow data to be analyzed in the context of existing knowledge. Use of context to modify analysis procedures is another area not commonly found in information analysis.

Fourth, the architecture explicitly deals with uncertainty by generating and testing competing hypotheses for unusual signals. This approach builds in a defense against prematurely accepting an explanation for a phenomenon.[6]

Finally, the architecture enables the collaboration of personnel needed to connect the dots, even if the personnel are distributed across different groups and agencies. The architecture looks not just for out-of-the-ordinary data but also for *out-of-the-ordinary analyses on the data*. Flagging these analyses can bring together groups of people who jointly are able to characterize a previously mysterious phenomenon. To date, we are not aware of other systems that examine analyses in this way.

Near-Term Implementation of ASAP

Fully implementing the ASAP architecture—especially with automated analysis components—would be a lengthy, multiyear process. However, several ASAP activities could be implemented quickly and would provide noticeable benefits. These would effectively allow human analysts' interactions to partially substitute for the automated agents described previously.

Each organization would need to work within its own cultural and organizational norms, bearing in mind that collaboration yields the greatest benefits for all. Not every recommendation we propose below would feel normal or natural to all participants. But we believe this is a feasible way to jump-start the ASAP analytical process.

We have emphasized the importance of detecting out-of-the-ordinary phenomena. A major requirement is understanding what constitutes "ordinary" and what types of behaviors are significant deviations from the ordinary. To make that judgment, one must first establish a baseline of ordinary patterns and behavior—canonical forms, as it were.

After identifying potential user communities for ASAP (intelligence, law enforcement, homeland security), we suggest, as a first step, formation of a representative *core* or *pilot group* that would draft

---

[6] DARPA's Project Genoa II (see DARPA Information Awareness Office, 2003b) provides tools to help analysts explicitly record, marshal evidence for, and test hypotheses; however, these tools do not appear to be explicitly linked to TIA's data analysis activities.

short (e.g., 2–4 page) example profiles for key behaviors and patterns. Some of these profiles would be for established asymmetric threats, such as suicide bombings; they would address the "life cycle" of the behavior or pattern discussed earlier as well as what threats commonly look like (terror attacks, terror support activities, etc.). Another, equally important set of profiles would capture what the status-quo conditions look like in watched domains such as international commerce, transportation, demolition, and infectious diseases; these profiles would help security professionals identify what observed behavior is truly out of the ordinary. It is important to note that these brief profiles are in no way intended to be comprehensive; they are merely meant to help analysts and field professionals in one domain educate their counterparts in other domains, in a much more intentional and systematic way than is done now, about what behavior to look out for.

We assume that secure electronic collaboration will be available to some degree. The second step would be to establish a set of electronic posting boards, divided by subject domain, where people in the field can report unusual phenomena and see whether anyone else has been observing similar or related occurrences—in effect, functioning as detection and linking agents for their analyst colleagues. Analysts "on the home front" would provide feedback on observations and postings from those in the field, confirming or redirecting their observations. Moderators trained in the domain(s) would then review the posting boards, selecting especially curious and significant reports to post to filtered boards that would be widely read by analysts. We recognize that potential organizational or cultural issues could limit the effectiveness of such an arrangement, yet we believe an open-minded, flexible approach will yield great dividends.

For such a system to be effective, users must be confident that they have something worthy of posting. It is common practice for field elements to take their direction from headquarters units in terms of requirements; this practice effectively tasks those in the field concerning collection requirements and is a well-oiled process with necessary information distribution and feedback mechanisms. After information responsive to those requirements has been submitted, the requirements are updated, modified or discarded. The same practice could be used for disseminating descriptions of out-of-the-ordinary signals that may be worthy of further investigation.

Personnel would initially post their informal analyses and questions to the unmoderated boards. It is important that the posting be voluntary yet be encouraged by colleagues and management. Publishing the profiles, case studies of successes resulting from posting, and case studies of successes resulting from other collaborative community efforts might encourage the shy and retiring to contribute—and also persuade the skeptics. It is important to create an environment and culture in which contributors do not feel vulnerable and exposed by posting what seems, from their perspective, to be out of the ordinary. Traditionally, intelligence and law enforcement professionals have been loath to share their information and insights given the risks of leaks, compromise, exposure, and failure. The unmoderated posting should be hosted in a secure environment and be benign, nonthreatening, and, if necessary, anonymous. Currently, some analysts, not wanting to show their hand, wait until they believe they have every last tidbit of information before laying their cards on the table. ASAP posting boards would discourage hoarding and encourage the posting of information that may not seem complete to an analyst but that could be valuable because it confirms data known to other analysts or colleagues in the field. It is important to generate an atmosphere of support among peers instead of competition or paranoia; messages sent by management to encourage posting would reinforce that sense of mutual support. We assume that all appropriate security and privacy policies would be strictly enforced in these forums. Between the profile-generation and iterative requirements process, field and other professionals should feel confident to submit their interpretations of out-of-the-ordinary events.

The goal of these boards is to develop a "virtual community" of intelligence, law enforcement, and homeland security professionals. Perhaps the most apt example of the community we would like to establish can be found in the online gaming world. We refer, particularly, to what are known as cooperative alternate reality games (cooperative ARGs). In these games, large groups of people—in some cases, thousands—become participants in an ongoing story. Advancing the story requires jointly collaborating to solve a sequence of puzzles that, when solved, reveal something that furthers the narrative (a web page, email address, phone number to call, etc.) Importantly, solving the puzzles requires a number of different skills.

In perhaps the most notable example to date, "The Beast" (developed by Microsoft to promote the movie *A.I.*; the plot had to do with solving a murder),[7] the puzzles ranged from interpreting lute music to building clay models of an island chain to decrypting ENIGMA-encoded messages. The largest group working on "The Beast," named "Cloudmakers," had over seven thousand members. To coordinate its members, Cloudmakers maintained a number of tools, accessible via its home page at http://www.cloudmakers.org:

- A generic posting board that allowed members to post any information related to the puzzles as well as clearly marked "speculations" on how a puzzle might be solved or where the narrative was leading.
- A moderated posting board that contained reprints of general-board posts felt to be of particular significance.
- An "official" posting board that contained only the most significant posts (announcements of group meetings in different cities, major game developments, etc.)
- A "game trail" that listed every puzzle discovered in the game, along with major developments used to solve the puzzle and every solution.
- A "guide" document that described, in narrative form, the process of solving the puzzles and walking through the story.

An important note is that all of the above tools contained hyperlinks as needed, to particular puzzle or solution pages, particular notes, sets of observed pages leading to solutions, and so on. The re-

---

[7] See, for example, Farhad Manjoo, "AI: Unraveling the Mysteries," *Wired News*, June 28, 2001, and Daniel Sieberg, "Reality Blurs, Hype Builds with Web 'A.I.' Game," CNN.com, June 13, 2001.

sult was a dynamic network of information, not a static chat room. A similar tool, the weblog (not used by Cloudmakers but in widespread use today) could be used in the ASAP schema to report on the most significant observations, and speculations on observations, in reverse chronological order.[8]

All these tools could be appropriated for intelligence or security applications, with open boards, moderated boards, trails, and guides established to look at particular terrorist organizations or potential threats. An additional complication is that, since there would likely be multiple virtual communities (not just a single game to monitor), the moderators would need to monitor multiple boards and make appropriate cross-posts between boards. The moderators would also have to be well versed in the legal and policy aspects of the information that shows up on the various boards.

The third step would be to develop tools that help personnel to identify posts relevant to what they have been observing. One might first implement organizational tools, beyond those discussed above, that would divide the posts into threads dedicated to particular occurrences and create indices of those threads. Particularly important threads would be associated with tailored journals summarizing key developments and current hypotheses; these journals could be regularly posted across threads and boards. The next step would to be create Google-like search engines for posts related to particular Boolean expressions. The final step would be the development of simple heuristics that look for connections and patterns across the threads of posted messages. Previously, we discussed agents that scanned analysts' reports for key phrases; something similar could be done to review message posts.

An Evolutionary Path for ASAP
We envision an organic growth pattern for ASAP systems. The first step in development would be to implement the above short-term recommendations. The next step would be to develop initial proto-

---

[8] For an introduction to weblogs, and a history, see Dave Winer, "The History of Weblogs," at http://newhome.weblogs.com/historyOfWeblogs.

types of the automated portions of ASAP. (Chapter Seven contains a research plan to develop these prototypes.)

Whether ASAP is initially implemented via the mostly manual boards-and-journals route or with automatic assistance, ASAP systems will begin small. They will start as pilot projects, probably in a single community of interest within an agency. From there, we envision adding new communities of interest in an organic (or geometric) growth pattern—adding a few additional communities at first, then more at increasing rates, until, eventually, large portions of the homeland security community use some ASAP functionalities.

The functionality of ASAP systems will increase over time. The above description of short-term improvements describes a multiphase process—starting with the creation of behavioral profiles and eventually leading to simple agents scanning analysts' posts. In the longer term, automated agents would be developed in multiple generations, starting with simple, rules-based agents and trend detection agents that are strictly manually controlled. The second step would be to create elementary processor agents and linking agents. From there, developers would create more sophisticated detection, processor, and linking agents and would start to create the simple, pattern-matching (and pattern-deviation) agents used to generate and test simple hypotheses. Eventually, ASAP systems would incorporate advanced agents that used detailed statistical models to extract meaning from sets of out-of-the-ordinary behavior.

Summary of the Schema

Table 1.1 summarizes differences between the proposed schema and traditional methods of intelligence analysis. The table also compares a near-term, manual implementation of ASAP with a full implementation.

Table 1.1
The ASAP Schema

Traditional Analysis	ASAP Advantages	ASAP Near-Term Implementation	Full ASAP System Implementation
Focuses on previous patterns	Searches for out-of-the-ordinary behavior, allowing for detection of previously unseen threats	Core or pilot group	New communities added to electronic boards
Time pressure drives toward premature closure	Allows memory of hypotheses and data rejected by analysts	Drafting short profiles of existing asymmetric threats—e.g., suicide bombing	Incorporates entire homeland security community
Analysts mostly operate on basis of own experience and biases	Leaves key analytic choices with analysts	Drafting short profiles of status quo in such "watched" domains as international commerce	Detailed architecture for out-of-the-ordinary analysis
Search tools mostly weed out what doesn't fit pattern	Notices what analysts are watching and asking	Users post on unmoderated electronic boards	Formal specifications for detection, linking, and hypothesis agents
Analysts are isolated within own groups and agencies	Facilitates collaboration between analysts studying the same phenomena	Moderators connect across analysts and, when possible, organizations	Analysis processes integrated across organizations

Outline of the Monograph

The bulk of this document describes an architectural design that would implement the ASAP schema with the assistance of automated agents and analysis support tools.

- Chapter Two describes the types of data an ASAP system would collect and discusses potential sources of data.
- Chapter Three provides an overview of the ASAP architecture, focusing on the overall control of the system. In particular, it describes how the system identifies which out-of-the-ordinary findings are truly worth further investigation. It also discusses the roles of analysts and automated agents in an ASAP system.
- Chapter Four describes how the dots would be detected through the use of contextual rules that identify out-of-the-ordinary data.
- Chapter Five describes various methods for finding relationships between data elements and connecting the dots.
- Chapter Six describes techniques for generating hypotheses about the meaning of the data and testing those hypotheses.
- Chapter Seven summarizes the ASAP architecture and presents a research plan and recommendations for action.
- Appendix A presents the full case study of the "November 9th incident" that began the paper. It presents, in narrative form, all the key events and interactions that occurred before the incident. It also describes how an ASAP system might have improved the analysis of those key events, through both automated analysis and support for human analysis and interactions.
- Finally, Appendix B reviews existing systems and analytic tools that might either complement the ASAP architecture or help implement an ASAP system's components.

CHAPTER TWO

Data Analyzed in the ASAP Schema

This chapter discusses the types and sources of data likely to be analyzed in an ASAP system. It also discusses what types of data and analysis findings should be declared significant ("truly out of the ordinary") and worth further investigation.

Figure 2.1 shows the areas of the ASAP schema on which the chapter focuses—what information about watched entities is considered to be of interest and how that information is captured and represented within ASAP-system databases.

Types of Data

We have identified seven major types of data entities as having meaning for threat assessment:[1]

- *People.* Everyone who might be involved in an attack, from terrorist group leaders to assistants to those directly involved in carrying out an attack.
- *Money.* All accounts and funding streams that could enable an attack.

---

[1] These categories are based on the authors' experiences and are intended solely for explanatory purposes. They are not an official list and are not to be considered either exhaustive or drawn from an intelligence agency's official list.

Figure 2.1
Watched Entities and Intercepted Information

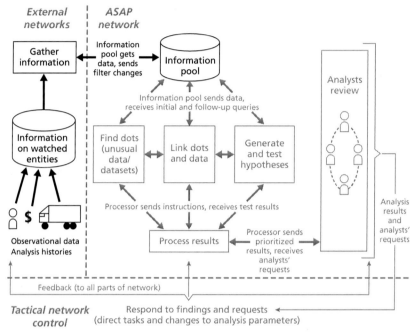

RAND*MG126-2.1*

- *Materiel.* All weapons, explosives, and other equipment that might be used to prepare or execute an attack.
- *Transportation.* All vehicles that could be used to move people and materiel and all vehicles used directly in an attack.
- *Accommodations.* All lodgings (apartments, hotels, etc.) used by people who might be involved in an attack.
- *Sustenance.* All consumable supplies, notably food and medicine, used by people who might be involved in an attack.
- *Communications.* All channels used by people involved in an attack to exchange information. We include in the definition of *channels* both the people who are communicating with each other and what modes they are using (phone, email, personal meetings).

A set of *attributes* is tracked for each of these core entities. For example, a *person* would be associated with an identity, current location, movement history, and activity history. Entities can also be *associated* or *linked* with each other; for instance, a person could be associated with a funding source and a means of transportation.

Sources of Data

The sources of information the ASAP system incorporates is a matter of policy debate. Substantial deliberations will be needed to balance effectiveness with security and privacy concerns. We have identified several major categories of sources.

Intelligence Networks

The core data-source category comprises existing intelligence streams identified as potentially having relevance to asymmetric threat assessment. As discussed earlier, however, receiving information from multiple intelligence sources (especially across agencies) involves crossing a number of technical, organizational, and procedural barriers, as well as ensuring that security and privacy regulations are upheld.

We envision first installing the ASAP system within a single intelligence agency, in which case the system would be presumed to have access to data on most agency networks. Multiagency ASAP systems would follow later. The latter systems would allow for the greatest analytic breakthroughs in connecting the dots because they would permit cross-agency data connections that are currently impossible. The legal and information security issues, however, would be much more complex.

From a technical perspective, the ASAP system would be granted access to particular intelligence networks by the network administrators, who would install interceptor agents within their systems and adjust the interception criteria in accordance with determined policy issues. Further, the ASAP interceptors could support much-finer-grained security provisions than simple access or non-access to networks. Administrators would be able to customize the information about particular data files that may be intercepted (for instance, only content, only metadata, only the fact the file exists), as well as to categorize the files that may be intercepted (by source, by region or intelligence topic, by processing thread, etc.).

Information Reported as Out of the Ordinary

Chapter One discussed how ASAP-like benefits could be obtained in the near term through the use of electronic bulletin boards allowing homeland security professionals to post out-of-the-ordinary information. Reports to these boards would be a key source of information for ASAP, especially with respect to domestic information.

Board reports would be an especially important source of *behavioral information*. In a number of places in future chapters, we reference particular types of observed behavior as being important indicators of asymmetric threats. As examples, we note how repeated videotaping of buildings at a level of detail virtually never done by tourists may indicate that people are casing those buildings. Similarly, we describe how people carrying around large numbers of cell phones and pagers outside of the buildings (so they can use each phone or pager only once, then discard it) may be members of terror groups planning an attack against the buildings. Such observations would enter ASAP through board posts from alert police and security guards; ASAP would not analyze hundreds of millions of cell-phone purchase records.

Applying automated agents to free-text reports of out-of-the-ordinary behavior will require those reports to be converted to sets of machine-interpretable data elements, using *natural language processing* techniques. A number of companies and organizations are building programs to do just that; Appendix B describes some of these programs.

Information on Critical Industries

We expect that a limited number of industries would be monitored as watched entities because of the nature of those industries. For example, hazardous materials (HAZMAT) production, handling, and transportation would be monitored to some extent, as would certain types of international commerce (already monitored by the U.S. Customs Service) and immigration patterns (already monitored by the Immigration and Naturalization Service). Similarly, certain types of law enforcement data might also enter ASAP, if law enforcement personnel could certify that the data warranted further investigation with respect to asymmetric attacks.

The types of data diverted to ASAP from these systems would obviously be a matter for significant policy debate. It would be consistent with existing security and privacy laws and regulations. An important note here is that diverted data would be on an "exception only" basis—only data meeting defined criteria for "warranting further analysis" would be reported. ASAP would not receive generic data streams from these systems. Not only will exception-only diversion policies provide inherently strong privacy and security protections, they will also help prevent ASAP systems from being overloaded.

Open-Source Information

Finally, we expect the previous information to be augmented with open-source information culled from the Internet. In general, given the privacy issues involved as well as the sheer volume of data on the Internet, we expect the roles of open-source data to be largely limited to the following:

- Review of media articles related to possible asymmetric attack plots (to identify people recently arrested, natures of plots discovered, etc.)
- Review of media articles pertaining to security issues related to potential targets for attack (for example, articles related to the HAZMAT industry, air transportation, bridge construction and maintenance)
- Review of posting boards and chat rooms frequently visited by terror group sympathizers (to identify social networks of poten-

tial sympathizers and to gauge the extent and nature of potential terror activity)

- Searches for open-source data to augment what is known about a particular entity (person, company, place, etc.) that has been flagged as being part of out-of-the-ordinary phenomena.

Commercial Databases

Commercial databases have a limited but important role in the ASAP architecture—they are used in the schema's backsweeping function, in which investigators seek information about particular people assessed as being suspects in a plotted asymmetric attack. The purpose of such backsweeping is to identify entities of interest (such as residences, vehicles, travel, close associates) related to the asymmetric attack. Such information can be vitally important in assessing the nature of a plotted attack, and eventually preempting it.

Importantly, however, in the ASAP schema backsweeping of commercial databases is not performed without probable cause to search the target of the backsweeping. Thus, for example, the schema complies with the proposed Citizens' Protection in Federal Databases Act, which would prohibit accessing databases "based solely on a hypothetical scenario or hypothetical supposition of who may commit a crime or pose a threat to national security." Consequently, because it would involve substantial human involvement (in the form of a court order), backsweeping of commercial databases would not be performed automatically.

Partitioning Intelligence and Domestic Investigative Data

Federal law requires that intelligence information be kept separate from law enforcement information, except in particular situations in which intelligence information is used as the basis for a criminal investigation. This partition will be maintained in the databases within an ASAP system. We envision having two major databases. The first would collect intelligence information and perform analysis on it. Entities of interest resulting from intelligence analysis would be passed (in accordance with applicable laws) to the second database, which collects and analyzes domestic information for the purpose of pre-empting domestic attacks.

CHAPTER THREE

The Atypical Signal Analysis and Processing Architecture

In this chapter, we provide an overview of an architectural design to implement the ASAP schema. We discuss the control structure of the architecture and describe the multiple layers of control that seek to ensure operational performance and, more broadly, allow the architecture to adapt over time. Finally, we compare the roles of analysts and automated software agents within the architecture. Successive chapters examine specific functional components within the architecture.

The Scope of an ASAP System

As with all major information analysis systems, the scope and complexity of an ASAP system is a vital issue. The size of the system—in terms of both the amount of data in the system and the number and complexity of the software agents working on the data—must be manageable.

With regard to the amount of data, the advantage of ASAP systems is that they work on data specifically diverted to the system because they meet specified filtering criteria; the ASAP architecture does not support the general copying of source databases into an ASAP system. Thus, we envision ASAP systems working with data volumes on the scales of millions of records with hundreds of millions of links; this range is well within existing database system capabilities. The situation is different for ASAP interceptor agents, which would have to filter very large streams of data or search very large databases for records matching particular criteria. The key for these interceptor agents is simplicity. Most of the interceptor agents, for example, would work by matching individual data with filter parameters rather than performing complex analyses.

It is important to control the number of system software agents, for several reasons. One reason is the sheer challenge of creating and maintaining the array of agents. Another is that, as the number of agents—and their interactions—increases, the analysis processes become so complicated that they are unpredictable and untraceable. Therefore, we envision controlling the complexity of the software agents in several ways. First, especially in early ASAP systems, the agents themselves would be fairly simple, largely based on simple parameter-matching and graph-algorithm heuristics. Second, the agents themselves would tend to follow common templates, with a few variables for the specific data fields to be compared and the specific rules governing the analysis. We envision at most a few tens of basic templates and perhaps a few thousand distinct agents operating in the system at any time. These agents would be carefully organized and tailored to the functions they serve and the ranges of data on which they operate; as a result, any particular data object might be subject to at most a few tens of agents. Thus, the processor agents, which assign incoming data objects to the appropriate detection agents, would be an important part of the control system.[1]

---

[1] Traditional descriptions of agent-based systems present "mobile" software agents "crawling around the network, searching for data to work on." In practice, effective agent-based systems do not work this way. COUGAAR, for instance (see Cougaar Group, 2002), employs a sophisticated scheduling system to match software agents to data objects and to determine both when those agents run and what data objects the agents work on.

Levels of Analysis in the ASAP Architecture

Two traditional methods are widely used in analyzing intelligence data: data mining and pattern analysis. Data mining looks for statistical relationships between data elements. Typically, these relationships are "discovered" entirely by data mining algorithms; previously known relationships are not taken into account. Consequently, the algorithms need large amounts of similar, complete data to find statistically significant relationships from scratch—which presents difficulties in the highly diverse and increasingly noisy world of asymmetric threat information. Conversely, pattern analysis scans data for pre-established patterns indicative of known and meaningful relationships. With pattern recognition, one finds exactly the signals one searches for. Unfortunately, many asymmetric threats do not obey standard patterns closely enough to be detected until it is too late.

In their traditional form, these two techniques are very good for detecting and isolating certain types of intelligence data. However, they have limits. Data mining is not well suited to events and data that are spread in time and space and that are few in number.[2] Pattern analysis is incapable of detecting either changes in patterns or patterns that are dynamic and ill defined.[3]

It is important to note that both of these methods fail to exploit analysts' expectations about what might be (or might not be) observed and the meanings of the observations. Our architectural design

---

[2] Traditionally, data mining algorithms seek to segment a large population into clusters, with some clusters having a greater likelihood of possessing a particular attribute. For example, one might attempt to identify people who will have a 2 percent chance of responding to a catalog mailing rather than a 0.1 percent chance. For a general introduction to data mining, the major techniques, and its uses, see the IBM International Technical Support Organization book on the subject (Cabena et al., 1998). Although data mining algorithms are a boon in marketing, the clusters they find would likely be too weak for asymmetric threat assessment, which needs to identify particular people likely involved in planned attacks.

[3] The books *Artificial Intelligence* (Rich, 1983) and *Machine Learning* (Carbonell, ed., 1990) discuss the difficulties of pattern-matching in such "routine" activities as text recognition (difficulties in telling whether a particular shape or sound is an "a" or an "o", for instance) unless the inputs exactly match or do not match a specified pattern. It is a much greater challenge to determine whether incoming intelligence—data subject to great uncertainties and missing a great deal of context—is indicative of a threat.

explicitly monitors streams of data over time and compares those observations with expected values. Importantly, our expected values apply not only to known patterns of planned attacks but also correspond to normal routine behavior. The deviations from expected,
status-quo behavior are the *dots*. They indicate initial clues that have
latent potential for guiding more-detailed analysis, for justifying further watching, or for authorizing intervention. Detecting the raw in-
formational clues that arise from data streams on *watched entities*
forms the first level or dimension of ASAP processing.

In addition to their study of observed data, the analysts' actions
can yield important clues, and searching for these clues is the second
level of ASAP processing. What the analysts probe for, request information on, and when they do so can indicate a heightening level of
awareness and curiosity about something out of the ordinary. Suppose, for example, that an FBI field office suddenly begins searching
for records on a truck-driving school—something the field office does
not normally do. By flagging unusual "analysis behavior," one might
find that the FBI office was tracking a set of unusual students that
other agencies could connect with terrorist organizations.

Finally, conventional data-mining and pattern-matching approaches fail to exploit key indications that come from analysts' notes
and reports. Analyzing these notes and reports is the third level of
ASAP processing. Using the analysts' written records, pieces can be
put together across reports and across analysts. For example, one
might find the aforementioned FBI field office and a CIA counter
terrorism group are both writing reports about members of the same
family—a fact of significant importance in detecting and understanding potential threats.[4]

---

[4] Note that the ASAP architectural design does not depend heavily on being able to interpret
analysts' notes. We recognize that parsing analysts' reports is a major technical challenge.
Nonetheless, we can envision simple algorithms, such as key-phrase search engines, that at
least determine if analysts are working on a particular topic.

Major Functional Components Within the Architecture

Data Interception, Storage, and Distribution

The three levels of processing imply that an ASAP system probes for data at various points throughout intelligence collection and analysis processes. The ASAP system uses a series of *interceptor agents* to filter data on the outside network and to divert relevant data for further review. At the first level, the interceptors filter raw streams of incoming data, intercepting data found to be applicable to the watched entities for further analysis. At the second level, the interceptors review data on how intelligence systems are used—who requests what, what probes are set, when they are set, who gets the information, and so forth. Finally, at the third level, the interceptors filter the basic results of information processing, translation, and any generated reports and notes based on the information. If the ASAP system is to detect the clues and perform a value-added task, it cannot have restricted vision of the types of information it reviews. The interceptors must be able to review a complete range of information from intelligence networks—including such metadata information as signal sources and the envelope (header and related information), not just the contents of the data, as well as system use and reports data. Figure 3.1 shows an ASAP interceptor diverting a variety of information for further analysis.

The interceptors are the only elements of the ASAP detector that sit on the information backbone. Analysis of data on the backbone must be done in a nonobtrusive fashion and should degrade the performance of the backbone as little as possible. This decoupling adds strength to the architecture because the backbone and detection system can evolve independently and be run separately as required.

Thorough and efficient data interception at various points throughout the intelligence process is the necessary first step of ASAP analysis. The intercepted data are tagged and assigned to their corresponding watched entities. Each data object must be associated with some entity, and that entity has a life-cycle model and data reposi-

Figure 3.1

Intercepting Data

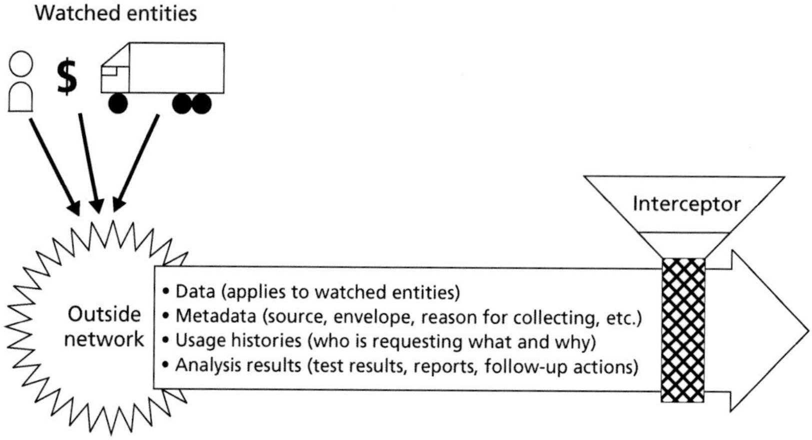

Watched entities

Outside network
- Data (applies to watched entities)
- Metadata (source, envelope, reason for collecting, etc.)
- Usage histories (who is requesting what and why)
- Analysis results (test results, reports, follow-up actions)

Interceptor

RAND*MG126-3.1*

tory. (We have already discussed the types of entities supported by the ASAP architecture in Chapter Two.) Figure 3.2 shows how the interceptors feed data to distributor agents, which in turn forward the data to appropriate *databases of watched entities* that associate the data objects with their corresponding entities.

The age of data objects would be noted, and the data automatically cleaned based on their temporal persistence. For example, monetary transactions for a specific organization may be tracked and cataloged for a rolling three-year period. The ASAP architecture emphasizes maintaining historical data because these data provide information about norms and expectations and can be used to pick up changes to the status quo. The maintenance of historical data also helps protect against introducing biases concerning what sorts of threats can be detected by tightly limiting analysis to a small set of previous "findings."

Finding Dots

One or more specialized *detection agents* then review the intercepted and stored data objects. These agents use data filter models to process

Figure 3.2
Data Sorting, Distribution, and Storage

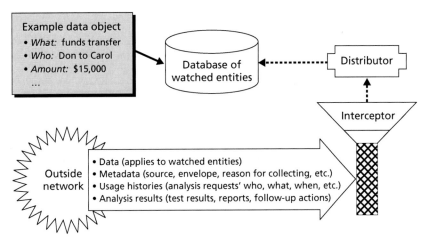

RAND*MG126-3.2*

the incoming data. The purpose of these agents is to identify the out-of-the-ordinary data objects (and sets of data objects) that are worth further attention—the *dots*. The detection agents would be specialized and tailored to process specific domains, such as transportation, financial transactions, and hazardous material.

Detection agents analyze data objects in two ways: reviewing the object's contents and its metadata. For example, the contents of an intercepted email transmission would be analyzed, as would the basic to-from and date information regarding the interaction that triggered the interception of the transmission.

In addition, detection agents analyze a data object's data and metadata with respect to *life-cycle models*. The data object pertains to some entity being watched, and this entity is in a certain state within its expected life cycle. For example, if a terrorist organization is known to be in a training phase, certain expectations would be normal for data traffic and personnel movement. These expectations would be different once the organization disperses after training. (Chapter Four discusses life-cycle models in more detail.)

Detection agents fall into two classes: *rules agents,* which look at single data objects (or small sets of data objects), and *trend agents,* which look at time series of data objects. For example, consider the analysis of funds transfers. A rules agent might search for single transactions associated with a particular entity that are more than $10,000, whereas a trend agent might determine whether the total level of funding has changed by more than 20 percent over the past two months.

Both types of agents employ *contextual rules* to test the data. Chapter Four discusses contextual rules in detail, but the key idea is that contextual rules can change as knowledge of the environment changes. For example, suppose a system receives information that a plot is under way to launch an attack against a major port in the northeastern United States; observations of unusual behavior in these ports would be treated with much greater scrutiny than they normally would.

Much of the incoming information is not in a form directly accessible by detection agents. Thus, *preprocessor agents* prepare the data objects to be analyzed by detector agents. For example, preprocessor agents compile data objects into time-series structures that can be analyzed by trend agents. Preprocessor agents can also perform basic linking of data objects—associating data objects with their entities, for example—so that rules agents can analyze the data objects properly.

Figure 3.3 shows an example of detector and preprocessor agents applied to a data object (a $15,000 funds transaction). The rules agent tests the object (on its own) to see whether it is more than some variable x. Suppose x is $10,000; then the rule is satisfied, and the agent declares the object to be a dot. In addition, the preprocessor agent places the data object into a series tracking funding transfers over time, and the trend agent tests whether the volume of transfers has changed significantly over the past two weeks. If this condition is satisfied, the agent declares the series (including the $15,000 agent) to be a dot.

Figure 3.3
Two Approaches to Detecting Dots

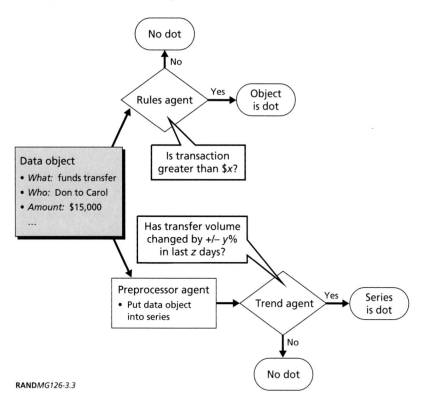

RAND*MG126-3.3*

The ASAP architecture uses four major significance levels in assessing software agents' test results: (1) below the threshold for further action (not a dot), (2) *mildly unusual* but not noteworthy in its own right, (3) *somewhat unusual* and worthy of further analysis, and (4) *highly unusual,* with the dot being given a high priority setting and broadcast to analysts throughout the system as specified.

Linking Dots

As noted, linking agents are responsible for finding additional information related to dots. These agents are divided into two categories:

first-order and second-order. *First-order agents* search the database of watched entities for additional data directly linked to the data objects making up the dot. *Second-order agents* search wider and deeper, looking for events, trends, or patterns of events similar to the dot.

Figure 3.4 shows an example of a processor agent calling for first- and second-order linking agents on a dot—namely, a $15,000 funds transfer from Don to Carol. The first-order agent assembles and links any data it can find on Don and Carol, such as associates, homes, vehicles, known organizational memberships, and travel movements (and plans, if known). The emphasis here is on identifying information on Don and Carol that is in the database of watched entities but that was previously excluded as being unimportant. The second-order agent assembles and links any data it can find on large funds transfers similar to the Don-to-Carol transaction. The results of the linking agents are sent back to the processor agent. In addition to calling for follow-up studies (see next section), the processor agent forwards the results to a reporting agent, which transmits the results to analysts.

Suppose the dot being tested was not the Don-to-Carol transaction but a major increase in funds transfers over the past two weeks within a particular region. In this case, a first-order agent would review trends in behavior within the region—whether people receiving the funds transfers were suddenly making travel plans or taking training classes, for example. Second-order agents would search for changes in funding transfers in other regions. Chapter Five discusses the techniques involved in linking data objects in some detail.

Generating and Testing Hypotheses

Hypothesis agents examine linked sets of dots and determine whether the dots match a pattern that provides evidence for, or weakens, a particular hypothesis. When analyzing a set of dots, the agents can either create a new hypothesis or test the dots against existing hypotheses. The primary role of the hypothesis and testing agents is to

Figure 3.4
Finding Data Related to Dots

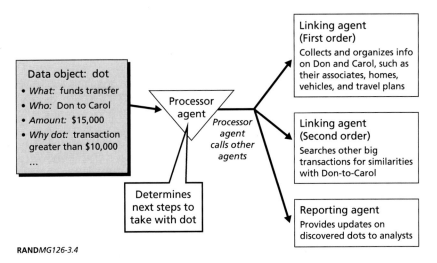

RAND*MG126-3.4*

assist analysts in determining what sets of atypical phenomena have the greatest priority for further investigation.

The ASAP architecture supports two broad classes of hypotheses. The first is specific—whether the pattern formed by the dots has some specific meaning for analysts, such as signals indicating a particular type of event against a particular target. We discuss hypothesis agents in detail in Chapter Six, but, in general, agents determine whether dots match specific templates to test specific hypotheses. For planned attacks, for example, hypothesis agents would look for data objects indicating particular targets combined with objects representing particular people, means of attack, and sponsoring terror organization.[5]

---

[5] The ASAP architecture described here, especially the hypotheses-generating and -testing components, is similar to "blackboard" designs used in artificial intelligence (see *PC AI Magazine,* 2002). Such systems place various data and hypotheses into a common blackboard database, to be interpreted and modified by rule-based agents. The structure can work extremely well in systems where the rule-based agents perform straightforward data-processing and analysis tasks. Note, for example, the success of the COUGAAR architecture, also a blackboard-based scheme, developed to generate detailed logistics plans (see Cougaar Group, 2002). In ASAP systems, processing would also be straightforward, even for hypothesis generation. Here, the primary role of the hypothesis agent would be to assess the "extent

The second, often more important class is nonspecific: The pattern formed by the dots is worth significant attention but lacks specific meaning. In general, agents test nonspecific hypotheses by seeing whether dot patterns violate templates describing expected, status-quo behavior. The ASAP architecture relies on a variety of nonspecific hypothesis agents tailored to process specific domains, such as transportation, financial transactions, and hazardous materials.

Figure 3.5 shows the process of generating a nonspecific hypothesis. Continuing the Don-to-Carol funds transfer example, a first-order linking agent produces a range of information about Don and Carol. The resulting linked data are submitted to a nonspecific hypothesis agent that looks for strongly out-of-the-ordinary behavior in the HAZMAT sector, since one of the linked data objects indicates that Carol has taken a HAZMAT-related course. The agent then scans the data against a set of rules representing typical behavior in the HAZMAT area. In this case, the agent decides that the data warrant a rating of "highly unusual," since the data contain two elements violating the ordinary-behavior rules: Carol is a professional (a lawyer) seeking HAZMAT truck-driver training, which is extremely uncommon, and Carol has no previous involvement in the HAZMAT field (this industry tends to be insular). The rating is sent back to the processor agent, which immediately tasks a reporting agent to forward the rating and supporting data to analysts.

As follow-up reports related to Carol arrive, the hypothesis agent tests the reports against the hypothesis that Carol's enrollment is highly unusual. Should the reports indicate that Carol has legitimate career reasons for taking the course, the hypothesis would be weakened and eventually disappear. Should the reports raise further

---

of atypicality"—to help analysts determine which phenomena are to be investigated. These agents would not reach formal conclusions by themselves, although they might flag datasets matching templates assigned meaning by an analyst. As a result, the one major criticism against blackboard systems—that they have not lived up to their initial promise of providing human-like complex reasoning in such areas as natural language processing—does not apply. In ASAP systems, such reasoning is assigned to analysts.

Figure 3.5
Using Dots to Generate a Hypothesis

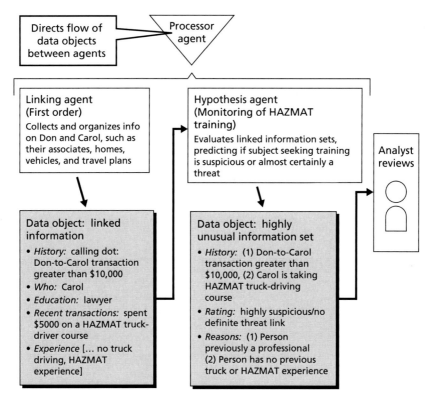

RAND*MG126-3.5*

suspicions, the hypothesis would be strengthened. Examples of strengthening behavior include Carol engaging in further unusual behavior (posting to terror-related chat rooms, for instance) or multiple people engaging in behavior similar to Carol's (multiple professionals taking HAZMAT-related classes, for instance).

Control of the ASAP Architecture

Principles and Structures of Control

ASAP's control structures allow for true context-dependent analysis, such that the activities used to analyze a set of data at any stage depend on what has been learned about the dataset to date, as well as other relevant environmental factors. ASAP networks would be controlled using principles and structures of *mission management*, which is the systemic control of distributed information networks in order to meet user and mission needs. Hollywood and McKay (forthcoming) have developed a detailed control framework for mission management.

The framework (and thus the control of ASAP systems) is based on four key principles of cybernetics, which is the formal study of change and control of change (see Ashby, 1956). The first principle is that, to control the system, one must understand both a system's individual pieces and the coupling between the pieces. Thus, the framework identifies and controls the end-to-end processes producing information in an ASAP system, starting from the initial interception of information through the delivery of completed reports to the analyst. Figure 3.6 shows an end-to-end, generic ASAP process. Note that the process diagram includes both direct processing flows and control and feedback flows.

The second cybernetics principle is that one cannot describe a system's evolution unless one has concepts—and variables or data structures representing those concepts—that accurately represent the state of the system. In the case of mission management, we require a data structure that reasonably represents the current status of the end-to-end information process, both for individual process activities and for the process as a whole. We employ *augmented process maps*, which associate activities in the process diagram—and the overall process—with tailored sets of performance metrics. The metrics are both quan-

Figure 3.6
Diagram of an End-to-End, Generic ASAP Process

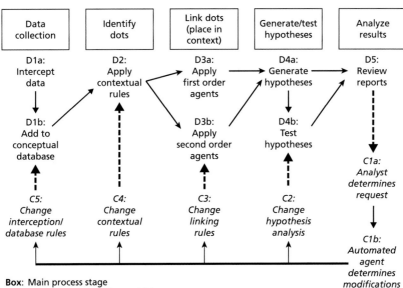

Box: Main process stage
D: Direct data-processing activities
C: Control/feedback activities

RAND*MG126-3.6*

titative (numerical) and qualitative (including, for instance, any known reasons that might explain the numerical measurements).[6] The augmented process map also describes any known relationships between measurements of process activity and the performance of the process as a whole.

Metrics within the mission management framework fall into five major categories. Table 3.1 describes the categories and presents sam-

---

[6] For example, a user satisfaction metric would provide a numerical indicator of a problem, the user's description of what the problem was, and the description and result of steps taken by network administrators to solve the problem.

Table 3.1
Example Performance Metrics for an ASAP System

Category of Metrics	Example ASAP Metrics
Quality	
Determines whether information provided is complete, relevant, accurate, and secure on a consistent basis	The percentage of information that should have been flagged by ASAP agents that is indeed flagged (based on statistical testing)
	The percentage of information flagged by ASAP agents that is found to be significant by ASAP analysts
	The percentage of information flagged by ASAP agents that was found to be insignificant (false positives)
	The percentage of ASAP system information accurately maintained with respect to the initially collected data
	The security of ASAP data, as measured by resistance to designed "red team" attacks
Quantity	
Determines whether the system can provide volumes of information when and where required	The percentage of intercepted information that the ASAP system is able to place in context and analyze using varying levels of ASAP agents
Timeliness	
Determines whether the end-to-end processing times meet users' due date requirements	The time from when a significant data element enters the system to the time it is employed in a report to an analyst
Mix and Variety	
Determine whether the network can quickly create or modify streams of information in response to user requests or other environmental changes	The range of requests for a new or modified stream that the system can accommodate
	The time required to create a new or modified stream
Analysis and Collaboration Support	
Determines whether users receive information in employable formats and whether the network provides sufficient tools for the users to collaborate	The percentage of information immediately employable by ASAP analysts
	The percentage of ASAP analysts reachable by any particular analyst

ple metrics for an ASAP system within each category. The actual metrics used would depend on the particulars of the ASAP system.

The third cybernetics principle is that, while one needs to take into consideration all types of information transactions and transformations inside a system to control the system, one does not need to take into account the specific media and physical processes used. Thus, for monitoring the inputs and outputs of agents in ASAP, we rely on general metrics that do not depend on the technical details of the agents or the supporting physical network—as presented, for example, in Table 3.1. Similarly, control of ASAP agents and the marshaling of data objects are based on general rules that treat individual ASAP agents and data objects as "black boxes."

The fourth cybernetics principle is that, in order to control a system, one needs to understand, collect data on, and have control mechanisms for all of the degrees of freedom of that system. Since an ASAP system is quite complex and must adapt to an ever-changing geopolitical environment in ways difficult to predict, being able to control all possible degrees of freedom is impossible. Thus, flexibility and adaptability in control is paramount.

Combining the above four principles yields the overall structure of the ASAP control system. At any time, the system maintains augmented process maps of the information flows within the system and tracks performance metrics for each process activity (both automated-agent and manual). A hierarchy of control agents oversees the workings of the process, attempting to keep performance metrics within desired parameters. We expect three types of electronic agents to be involved in the operational control [7] of ASAP systems: processing agents, which directly marshal sets of data objects in response to the objects' metadata and analysis results; automated control agents, which allocate resources and control processing flows in response to demands for particular types of information; and control assistance agents, which assist ASAP network managers in modifying the system

---

[7] The mission management framework developed by Hollywood and McKay also incorporates control elements responsible for systems engineering and architectural decisionmaking; however, such higher-layer control elements are outside the scope of this document.

in response to issues outside the domain of the automated agents. (Control assistance agents notify managers of network problems, give context to the problems, and provide communications and control tools for helping the managers isolate and fix problems.)

All three types of agents employ a set of control logic rules to make decisions. The rules operate using inputs from data objects or system messages requesting a control decision, system status information from the augmented process maps, and the internal state of the control agent. The rule sets can resemble a classic stimulus-response table ("if X then Y"), a finite state diagram, or a complicated decision tree, depending on what is appropriate for the control agent. It is important to note that these rule sets may be modified dynamically in response to changing environmental situations simply by having a control agent execute a rule to change the control logic. For example, an automated control agent, when faced with a flood of incoming data objects, can change the rules used to determine which level of analysis should be performed on a data object—in this case, reducing sensitivity to avoid overloading the system.

Note that the exact nature of the control structure used in an ASAP system—the process maps and metrics employed, the types of control agents used, the structures of the control logic used, and the exact mechanics of carrying out the marshaling of data objects and the modification of system elements and flows—would be a major focus of any future development of the ASAP concept.

Control of ASAP systems takes place at two fundamental levels: the operations level and the tactical level. The purpose of operations-level control is to guide data through the various analytic functions, ensuring that the data are properly characterized. The purpose of the tactical level is to ensure that the system as a whole can respond appropriately to environmental changes. Surrounding the direct control of the ASAP system are learning processes, which help the system adapt to improve performance over time.

Control at the Operations Level

Operations-level control in ASAP is the domain of the processor agent, as directed by analysts' requests. Figure 3.7 highlights these two segments of the ASAP schema.

General Principles. Operations-level control is *rule-based* and *context-dependent.* That is, decisions as to what tests to execute next and how to interpret the results use the following types of information as input:

- information about the data being analyzed
- information about the analyses previously performed and the results of those analyses

Figure 3.7
Operational Control in the ASAP Schema

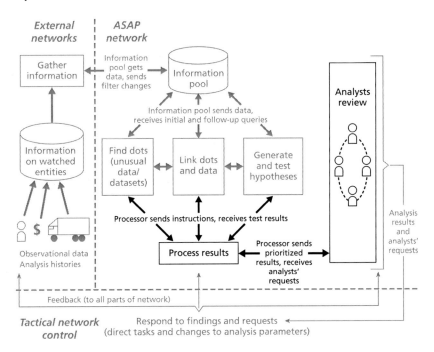

- information about the hypotheses being tested against the data and the current strengths of those hypotheses.

The above inputs are complemented by information about the "who, what, when, why, where, and how" of the information being analyzed, the mission or task associated with the analysis, and the analysts requiring the analysis. These combined dimensions define the control structures needed to make sense of what is ordinary and what is out of the ordinary.

The Processor Agent. The processor agent is the core instrument of operations-level control. Data objects (and sets of data objects) triggering the mildly unusual, somewhat unusual, or highly unusual detection—the dots—are transmitted to a processor agent. As the nerve center of the ASAP analysis process, the processor agent's purpose is to determine what to do when it receives the dot. The processor agent has two major responsibilities.

The first responsibility is to call agents to perform follow-up tests on the dot. The processor agent calls linking agents to search for information potentially related to the dot (in the backsweeping process). It also calls hypothesis agents to determine whether dots—and any related dots and data found via the linking agents—match patterns that strengthen or weaken particular hypotheses. Any connections or matched hypotheses found would trigger additional backsweeping and hypothesis-testing. This processor agent–directed process is then iterated, with more and greater-priority results triggering more follow-on analysis.

The processor agent receives direction from two sources. The first is automated logic; finding a dot above a certain significance level might automatically trigger a corresponding backsweeping, for example. The second is manual; analysts can order the processor agent to call any ASAP query or test manually. At the operational level, analysts act on the ASAP network through requests to the processor agent.

The second responsibility of the processor agent is to prioritize the detected dots, reporting the higher-priority dots and analysis results to analysts. Any *highly unusual* items or dot connections found would trigger immediate notices to the appropriate analysts, informing them of the status and what further analyses have been automatically launched. Lower-priority items of note would be transmitted in a daily communication. Other dots (and data items) would be ignored. Factors considered in prioritizing dots are discussed below.

Note that while the processor agent calls linking, hypothesis, and reporting agents, the processor agent does not do any of the follow-up work itself. Instead, additional agents perform the specified functions with the processor agent in a controlling role. This division of tasks allows for modularity and flexibility in determining what analyses should be performed on data elements.

Prioritization. Any large analysis system is likely to generate a very large number of potential "hits" (dots, in our case). Most of them would be false positives and must be filtered out of the system both for sheer feasibility (the U.S. government has limited resources to investigate dots) and to protect the privacy of people falsely detected. The scalability problem is further complicated for ASAP because of the architecture's use of distributed, semi-independent autonomous agents working on subsets of conceptual graphs; without careful attention, such approaches could lead to a combinatorial explosion in the number of false positives and analysis requests created.

The main complexity-control approach that we have identified is to rank-order the detected dots using a multidimensional priority scheme and allow low-priority hits to remain unanalyzed. From a practical perspective, we expect detected dots to fall into four categories: investigated by a human, investigated in detail by automated agents (multiple agents directly analyzing the single dot), indirectly addressed by automated agents (dot becomes a data point in trend agents), and not addressed at all (the bulk of the detections). Below are some likely candidates for dimensions to determine the rankings.

Connectivity. This type of rule applies to links between observations, especially potential dots. The more links there are to particular observations, or to particular entities that are the subject of the observations, the more significant the dot is likely to be. We can create similar rules for the number of agents declaring an observation (or set of observations) to be a dot. Here, the number of links can and should be weighted by the importance of other dots linking to the observation—for example, observations related to someone known to be a high-ranking operative of a terror group would be ranked higher than an observation related to someone only marginally and indirectly linked to the group. This approach is similar to how the Google search engine ranks pages: It counts the number of links to each page weighted by the predetermined importance of the linking page.[8]

Frequency. This type of rule applies to trends in observations and is particularly relevant to second-order agents tracking similarities in phenomena. It simply states that the more prevalent a phenomenon is (in terms of observations reporting it), or the more rapidly it appears or spreads, the more significant it is. For example, in the case study in the appendix, the sudden arrival of high-speed tuna boats in multiple harbors around the world is more significant than a surge in tuna boats in a single harbor.

Coverage. This type of rule generates a small number of dots for further analysis that are related to every currently known terror organization, geographic area, or watched process. The rule is designed to defend against the "fighting the last war" problem by ensuring that at least some attention is paid to potential future threats.

Commitment. This rule characterizes observations that show significant work or commitment as more important than an observation representing a discussion or note taken in passing. Example of a commitment rule would be to place observations demonstrating significant work in casing a target on a higher level than merely talking about a target. For example, ABC News reported on the existence of videotapes detailing al Qaeda operatives' personal surveillance of the World Trade Center, the Sears Tower, Disneyland, Universal Studios in Los Angeles, and the Golden Gate Bridge.[9] The much greater commitment shown to these places would cause ASAP to de-

---

[8] See Google's own explanation of its page-ranking scheme at http://www.google.com/technology/.

[9] "Videotape Shows Preparation for US Attacks—ABC," Reuters, March 4, 2003. See also Andy Soltis, "WTC Vid Declares Planning of Attack," *New York Post*, March 4, 2003, which also mentions surveillance of the Brooklyn Bridge, Wall Street, and the Statue of Liberty.

clare them to be at much greater risk than other places merely mentioned once or twice by al Qaeda operatives.

Oddness. For example, the managing director of Jane's Information Group noted that *Jane's Intelligence Review* (August 2001) remarked that al Qaeda was training commercial pilots.[10] ASAP would treat this information as being of high priority simply because of its strangeness with respect to normal profiles of terror organizations in general and al Qaeda in particular.

Context. Finally, this most important type of rule dynamically adjusts a dot's generic prioritization rating based on current environmental knowledge. The previous section contained an example of scrutinizing atypical behavior reports from HAZMAT truck-driving training courses given information indicating that a lawyer with no trucking experience was attending such a course; this is an example of a contextual prioritization rule.

Control at the Tactical Level

Tactical-level control concerns the modification of the ASAP agents and overall network processes to adapt to environmental changes. An ASAP system will support tactical control by making all agents and processes fully customizable. Which agents are used, what the agents' internal logic is, and what workflow-governing rules are used are all subject to change. The primary directors of an ASAP system are the analysts; ASAP systems use a fully open-loop control model, so that analysts have full authority to task agents, set testing criteria, and set priorities as they see fit. The analysts are assisted by automated control agents, which can automatically implement well-understood workflow and analysis changes. Figure 3.8 highlights the components of the ASAP schema responsible for tactical-level control.

---

[10] Alfred Rolington, "9/11: In Search of Context and Meaning," *Jane's International Security News*, September 11, 2002.

Figure 3.8
Tactical Control in the ASAP Schema

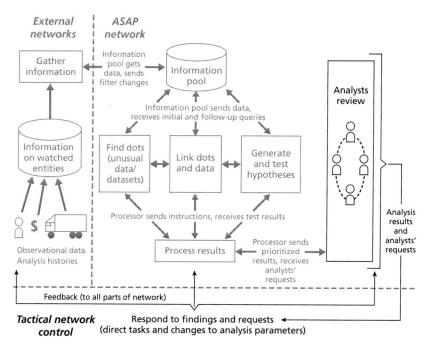

RAND*MG126-3.8*

Learning and Adaptation

An ASAP system must be able to learn and adapt over time if it is to react to environmental changes—especially changes caused by adversaries attempting to react to the system's successes. Learning is also important simply to improve the system's performance in detecting truly anomalous information while ignoring routine information. Below, we present several strategies for learning and adaptation: automated learning, manual adaptation processes, and periodic environmental reviews.

Automated Learning. Implementation of the linking, hypothesis-generating, and hypothesis-testing agents will require the use of data mining and pattern-recognition algorithms.[11] Both of these types of algorithms rely on statistical-training techniques. The details of statistical training are outside the scope of this document, but the basic idea is that we present linked sets of data to an algorithm, along with a statement of the set's significance. At base, *significance* is defined as whether or not the set is linked to threatening activity. One can also be more sophisticated, specifying whether the sets are linked to specific activities. The algorithms use these sets to develop rules estimating the probability that incoming datasets are significant or not; *significant* is defined in terms of how the algorithm was trained (linked to terror, linked to specific attacks, etc.). The rules thus generated are inserted into new agents to analyze incoming data.

Importantly—and here is where learning comes into play—statistical training also takes place using actual observational data, analysis histories, and analysts' reports. Thus, as certain activities are found to actually be related to planned attacks, data relating to those activities are fed to the training algorithms as "significant." Similarly, as certain unusual activities are found to be ordinary, related data are fed to the training algorithms as "not significant." Such learning can dramatically increase an ASAP system's effectiveness over time. Note, however, that automated learning largely refines existing detection tests; it does not create entirely new ones.

Manual Adaptation Processes. Any analysis system faces the problem of fighting the last war, in terms of what information is analyzed and what assumptions are used in the analyses. In ASAP systems, the problem is somewhat mitigated through the use of second-

---

[11] Although the agents would employ data-mining algorithms to filter data and match them to patterns, we reiterate that ASAP systems would not perform unguided data mining in the traditional sense. In conventional data mining, a set of dependent variables (in counterterrorism, for example, entities that were, or were not, associated with planned attacks) and a large set of independent variables (other characteristics about the entities) are fed into an algorithm, which must develop, *with no further information*, a set of rules that tend to associate independent variables with the dependent variables (e.g., terrorists tend to have certain demographics). ASAP, conversely, builds heavily on the existing knowledge of homeland security-related communities to create and maintain the detectors, patterns and priority rules (especially to create representations of what typical and atypical behavior look like). ASAP systems may support unguided data mining to discover rules that supplement the profiles, but such unguided data mining is strictly secondary.

order agents and other analysis tools that pick up truly odd behavior, even without a preexisting rule that the behavior constitutes a threat. ASAP's allowance of multiple, potentially disagreeing filters, tests, and perspectives also helps limit the problem. Nonetheless, the ASAP system will still face the problem simply because it makes explicit choices about what data to collect and what analyses to use.

Thus, it is important to allow those choices to adapt over time. As noted above, automated learning systems can refine the ASAP system's operations but cannot truly modify them. Manual adaptation processes that incorporate human learning and insight have that capability. A major feature of any ASAP implementation, then, is that modifying the system must be easy.

Two kinds of modification require system support. The first is modification of the types of data collected by the system, which requires both technical and process flexibility. On the technical side, the virtual machine–distributed agent architecture presented in this report is intended to isolate and cushion an ASAP system's functionality from particular data sources and formats. This should aid in the rapid introduction of new sources and data streams and should allow rapid redirection of data in a transparent fashion. On the process side, the organization that supports the ASAP system would need to have procedures in place to allow requests for new types and sources of data to be incorporated quickly. These procedures include

- a current and accessible catalog of the available major data sources and types. The catalog would include a contact list regarding where data access and modification requests should be submitted.
- standardized review and approval processes for data-addition and modification requests that would ensure that the request is (1) justified, (2) feasible, and (3) performed in compliance with security and privacy requirements
- in-place procedures for auditing and filtering the data exchanged with an ASAP system to ensure that it meets security and privacy requirements. Such procedures are especially important when sharing information outside of U.S. government sys-

tems—for example, exchanges between U.S. government and local authorities, foreign governments, and nongovernmental organizations.

The second class comprises changes to analysis tests performed within ASAP. Again, technical and process flexibility are required. On the process side, it needs to be easy for analysts to modify existing test agents and code new ones. On the technical side, it needs to be easy for administrators to review, validate, and approve proposed analysis changes in a timely manner.

Periodic Environmental Reviews. Even manual adaptation processes are insufficient defenses against the fighting-the-last-war problem because the changes requested on an operational basis tend to be natural extensions of the data currently collected and the analyses currently performed. To ensure "revolutionary" adaptations, an ASAP system would need processes to help identify those adaptations.

A periodic environmental review is one such process. In these reviews, panels of analysts, system customers, field agents and other information providers, and outside advisors (a security-cleared advisory group, for example) would be asked to

- scan the environment for major potential changes, with an emphasis on potentially emerging threats (e.g., "what aren't we looking at that might hurt us?") and the types of indicative signals those emerging threats might generate
- develop a list of information needs that would help monitor potential changes effectively
- evaluate how well those needs are being met with the current portfolio of data sources and analyses
- identify and develop sources of information and analysis needed to meet the needs.

The schedule, composition, and exact policies used in the review process would depend on the specifics of the ASAP system and the information providers, analysts, and clients using the system. Beyond period review processes, it would also be important to have in place some sort of standing review committee that could address proposals for major time-critical system changes.

Roles of Human Analysts and Automated Agents

As noted in the introduction, we envision the ASAP architecture as providing a valuable tool to analysts. It should in no way be seen as a substitute for human analysis. Instead, the automated components of ASAP would complement what humans do well and would provide a set of activities well suited to computers but poorly suited to humans:

- It would detect out-of-the-ordinary signals currently buried in the mountains of intelligence information collected every day—signals that human analysts cannot possibly review on their own.
- The system would find links between pieces of data in the mountains of information, a task that is even more difficult than reviewing each piece individually.
- By detecting significant trends over time, the system would help mitigate the "boiled frog syndrome" (the urban legend that a slowly heated frog will allow itself to be boiled alive) in which humans ignore changes that happen slowly but become very important over time.
- By detecting out-of-the-ordinary behavior that does not necessarily fit into patterns of previous attacks, the system can potentially detect entirely new threats. This helps avoid the fighting-the-last-war problem in which humans filter information specifically for indicators of previous events, ignoring signals of new threats.
- Finally, an ASAP system makes it much easier for analysts to follow up on detected out-of-the-ordinary behavior. The system automatically provides the analysts with a complete historical trace of all the data leading to the detection. It also provides links to those who collected or analyzed the data, facilitating collaboration.

Although there is a great deal of automation and support for the analyst, ASAP is just that: it is only a complement to the innate and intuitive skills the *human* analyst brings. Whether actively engaged in all aspects of ASAP or a casual user, the analyst would continue to have the essential role in an ASAP system. The automated agents can tell an analyst what signals are out of the ordinary, but they cannot say what the signals really mean. It is up to the analysts, with their unquantifiable but critical knowledge (personalities, organizational traits, third- and fourth-order influences on how organizations work, etc.) and their analytic insights, to provide understanding. The analysts would be the source of the definitions of what constitutes out-of-the-ordinary behavior to begin with. They would have the primary responsibility for determining the meaning of unusual phenomena and what actions should be taken in response. Consequently, the entire process would be dynamically controlled based on analysts' requests and commands.

No one would expect analysts to significantly change how they do business just to adopt a new semiautomated tool. However, there is bound to be an initial adjustment period for analysts as they use ASAP—primarily in terms of the analytic processes underpinning the system. Analysts would first need to consciously apply the basic concepts of systematically searching for the out of the ordinary and then determine what the discovered unusual information means, rather than looking for data that fall into particular categories. The analogy here is that ASAP systems analysts need to adopt the approach of Sherlock Holmes, who emphasized looking for "anything out of the ordinary routine of life."

Because ASAP supports collaborative work and its results are superior with collaboration, this process may introduce opportunities for new business practices or workflows. For example, as analysts seek to understand the meaning of reported dots and search for related information, they may often need to work with their colleagues to get the information and understanding they need.

Finally, the analytic organization would need to accept and reward risk-taking. Managers need to reward any significant contributions to the knowledge bases underlying the ASAP system, even if the contributions represent "failures" (following up on dots that turn out to be routine). In many cases, ruling out dots can be just as important as finding potential threats and can have added value if the reasons for dot exclusion are codified in the system. Thus, managers need to support a philosophy of "99 failures are acceptable as long as they produce one major success," assuming that the analysts are making good, honest, and reasonable efforts.

It is also important to have processes in place for learning from both successes and failures in connecting the dots. In addition to improving their system effectiveness in general, terrorist organizations have frequently carried out denial and deception operations against intelligence networks, and we can expect that they will attempt to make their real operations look ordinary while planting false "dots." However, both types of concealment require their own sets of out-of-the-ordinary activities. It is our belief that, through effective learning processes, ASAP can adapt to pick up unusual behavior indicating denial and deception.

CHAPTER FOUR

Finding the Dots

This chapter considers techniques for identifying which data objects are dots worth further investigation. Figure 4.1 shows the area of the ASAP schema on which the chapter focuses—the identification of the dots and the initial determination of what actions to take with the newly discovered dots.

Finding Dots with Rules

In general, we identify out-of-the-ordinary activities—the dots—by seeing if they meet some set of criteria, or *rules*. The rules fall into several categories.

- *Single-point analysis.* These rules apply to single data elements. For example, a rule might be to identify individual funds transactions greater than $10,000. (Continuing the discussion of data representations from Chapter Three, a single transaction would be an element of an object representing a general family of transactions—"Funds from Don," for example.)
- *Trend analysis.* These rules apply to a set of data elements tracking a phenomenon over time, called a *trace*. For example, a rule might be to detect changes in transfer volume greater than

Figure 4.1
Identification and Initial Processing of the Dots

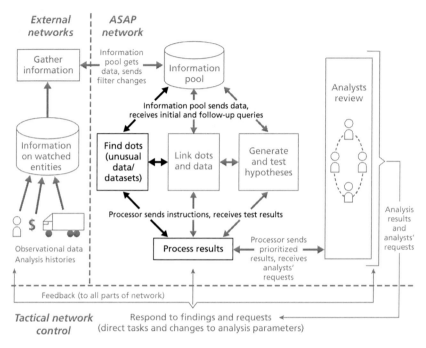

RAND*MG126-4.1*

50 percent. (Note that each trace has its own parent data object.)

- *Multipoint analysis.* These rules apply to a group of linked data objects and elements. For example, a rule might be to highlight relationships in which more than three people receive funds from the same person.

The sample rules above are static or generic rules—they apply equally to all data objects and elements in an ASAP system. However, such generic rules are of limited value. Given the huge amount of information in intelligence networks, generic rules will likely either produce huge numbers of false positives (if the rules are liberal) or miss critical signals (if the rules are strict). Analysts will need to increase the discrimination of dot-finding rules if they are to be effective.

As Alfred Rolington, Managing Director of Jane's Information Group, points out, the key to finding critical pieces of intelligence information is to use the *context* of the information.[1] We define *context* in accordance with *Webster's Collegiate Dictionary*: "the interrelated conditions in which something exists or occurs; [its] environment; setting." More specifically for our purposes in improving dot-finding rules, the context for a piece of information is a set of *contextual relationships* that link specifically to that datum. These relationships jointly interact with the datum by *changing the default rules* on how that entity should be regarded—making a seemingly routine observation much more significant than it would normally be, for example. Incorporating contextual relationships in dot-finding rules yields *contextual rules*.

Representing Context

A contextual rule first determines whether a data element's attributes meet a special set of criteria; if so, the rule applies a special set of criteria to that observation. For example, suppose Alice attempts to board a flight for nefarious purposes. She triggers some generic airline profiling rules, but weakly—buying a one-way ticket right before the flight, for example—but would likely board the flight successfully. However, suppose Alice was checked against an ASAP database supporting contextual rules and found to have asked questions in terrorist-frequented chat rooms about how to make and conceal explosives in clothing. Alice's attempt to board becomes much more unusual, and she would likely be held for questioning.

Contextual information is a critical booster of the power of threat assessment networks. It serves as a *signal booster,* helping identify people, places, and things that should be investigated, even if they

---

[1] Alfred Rolington, "9/11: In Search of Context and Meaning," *Jane's International Security News*, September 11, 2002.

do not register with the cruder, generic pattern testers. It also greatly reduces the number of false positives.

It is important that the implementation of contextual rules be dynamic, allowing this signal boosting to occur as the environment changes or as we learn more about the environment. Thus, discovery of one important dot triggers a cascade of other rules to find other, related dots. Implementing new rules is a primary mechanism for carrying out backsweeping, as well as for changing the criteria for scanning incoming data. For example, suppose that Alice was searched prior to boarding the plane and that her clothes were filled with explosives after all. This discovery would establish a new set of contextual rules: Any data observation related to Alice has high priority.

Dimensions of Context

To build contextual rules, we need a basic grammar of types of knowledge that will be put into the rules. We call these types of knowledge *dimensions of context.* These dimensions include tactical components of a terror attack (as with Alice's explosive clothing), strategic components of a terror attack or terror organization, and times and events that have meaning for a terrorist organization. The dimensions also describe ordinary behavior in key areas such as HAZMAT handling and international shipping.

Times, Events, and Behavioral Life Cycles

Time is an important variable for finding special-case rules. For example, changes in time of year make certain types of targets more or less valuable; similarly, different organizations might prefer to strike on particular dates or at particular events. Such knowledge makes observations related to those times and events particularly important.

Beyond particular known times and events, organized behaviors culminating in a major event (such as a terror attack) follow a fairly standard life cycle having several distinct phases. Analysts can significantly refine their searches for dots by understanding where in the life cycle a planned attack is and looking for data elements representative of that life-cycle phase. Figure 4.2 shows a typical life cycle of a terror attack, roughly graphing organizational activity by time.

Table 4.1 describes each of these phases and some corresponding contextual rules in more detail.

Structures of Tactical Behavior

Terror attacks have common structures, depending on the type of the attack. These structures can be exploited, creating special-case rules to determine whether observed behavior is consistent with attack preparations. In particular, we can create profiles describing the activities needed to carry out different types of attacks and when those activities might occur (referenced by whether they are initial, developing, operating, or pre-event activities). The contextual rules would then search for people carrying out those activities, emphasizing groups of people carrying out multiple activities fitting the profile.

Figure 4.2
Levels of Activity During the Life Cycle of a Terror Attack

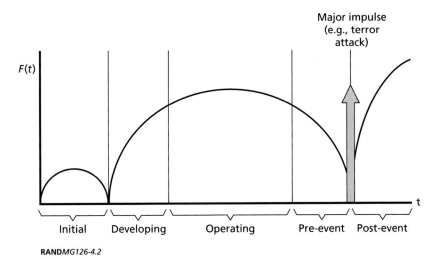

RANDMG126-4.2

Table 4.1

Contextual Rules Corresponding to Activity Life-Cycle Phases

Phase	Example Contextual Rules
Initial: High-level planning of terror attacks, usually at overseas "summits"	Following meeting, people linked to terror group may suddenly move to a common destination; people are likely involved in a planned attack, and common destination is a likely target or staging area. Summit attendees likely have some involvement in terror attacks.
Developing: Establishing of attack infrastructure, such as basing attack leaders in the U.S., providing them with covers, and setting up training and acquisition programs	New arrivals in U.S following an initial phase and those who seek out-of-the-ordinary jobs (especially related to attacks—HAZMAT, etc.) or who try especially hard to hide their existence may be involved in a terror attack
Operating: Actual training, material gathering, and material preparation for a terror attack	Same as above—continue monitoring people who arrived following initial terror phase and their jobs and training Examine contacts of unusual persons, especially new arrivals Search for persons casing targets or means of attack (people making studies/videotapes of buildings, airports, and the people in them that are more detailed than usual) Look for behavior symbolizing concealment (e.g., carrying around large numbers of cell phones and pagers, using cell phones exactly once before discarding them)
Pre-Event: Final preparations for terror attack	Look for major movements by suspected persons or anyone linked to a terror organization. Examples include quitting jobs, moving out of apartments, and booking remote travel Searches for casing behavior are particularly relevant
Post-Event: Terrorist organization repositions itself and its members following attack (prepares for follow-up attacks, military confrontations, etc.)	Search for people congratulating each other on the success of the attacks Search for people suddenly moving following the attack

For example, consider a truck bombing. This form of attack requires acquiring explosive materials, a truck, a place to construct the bomb, and the training of people to construct the bomb and drive it to its target. It also requires casing a target to a high level of detail, so that the driver knows exactly how to navigate any defenses. All of these activities are subject to detection.

Structures of Strategic and Organizational Behavior

The structure of terrorist organizational behavior and strategy can also be exploited. In particular, terrorist organizations have internal support functions that have to be carried out—internal communications, decisionmaking, recruiting, maintaining morale, and financing. Again, profiles describing the types of activities needed to carry out a communications web or a financing web can be created and tested against system data. Further, these profiles can and should be updated as more about a terrorist organization is learned. For example, the profiles describing al Qaeda operations would be much more detailed following months of interviewing detainees at Guantanamo Bay and elsewhere than they would have been initially.

Structures of the Status Quo

Perhaps the most important dimension of context is the status quo. Earlier, we described the use of non-indicative patterns; contextual rules are a primary way of implementing these out-of-the-ordinary patterns. But we can also create profiles describing how people normally behave in a variety of activities and search for people deviating from those profiles. As noted earlier, of particular interest are groups of people violating multiple status-quo relationships simultaneously.

As an example of a status-quo pattern, consider what factors might go into a status-quo pattern for ocean shipping (directly related to the scenario in the prologue):

- Any major increases or decreases in vessel traffic should depend on variances in demand for shipping or other known factors dictating large amounts of goods at particular times.
- Shipped items should pass what are known as *continuity checks*—items registered for shipping at the point of embarkation should arrive at the point of disembarkation, and items arriving at the point of disembarkation should have been registered at the point of disembarkation.
- Those organizations and persons most involved with shipping—the shipping companies, company executives, ship officers, and even laborers—should have substantial or verifiable histories with the industry.

Violations of the above factors are curious; multiple, related violations of the above factors (as described in Appendix A for the tuna boats) are clearly worth further investigation. We can create similar status-quo profiles for other forms of shipping, as well as for other industries and public activities with a direct relationship to terror attacks (HAZMAT, aircraft, tourism, etc.).

Structures That Disrupt: Dot Noise and Intentional Denial and Deception

We can expect, and have observed, terrorist organizations like al Qaeda using denial and deception techniques to attempt to conceal planned terror attacks and other organizational activities. Denial and deception, which can be thought of as intentionally filling data streams with bad data and noise, are a serious challenge for any intelligence analysis system, including the ASAP architecture. Attention must also be paid to false results and noise resulting in dot relationships being triggered and transmitted to the human analysts. ASAP would use the dot recognition and relationship capability in two ways in order to address intentional and unintentional noise.

For unintentional noise, the ASAP recognition and relationship logic could be applied to its own output in a second layer of analysis, seeking those dots and links that meet contextual rules for being noise. Dots indicated as noise would be filtered off the main ASAP system and rerouted to a specific analyst who would be responsible for reviewing blocked results. This is a concept similar to email filters.

The intentional efforts at deception and denial could be addressed partially by the ASAP contextual rules. Analysts could create and apply profiles for known techniques to employ denial and deception. It is not possible to catch and detect all instances of denial and deception, but it should be possible to identify and reduce the amount of noise passing through the system. As with detected dot noise, any denial and deception items could be routed to a specific individual (or group of analysts) for review. In terms of intentional denial and deception, detected efforts could even strengthen knowledge about suspected terror threats.

Consider some examples of what might go into denial and detection profiles:

- One might expect false attacks to be talked about loosely ("bragged about") over channels recognized as being monitored or when suspects are first interrogated. Conversely, information about real attacks, to the extent they must go over insecure channels, would be talked about very obliquely. For example, suppose a terrorist chat room contains much discussion of the impending doom to the West brought about by Albert and his cohorts, with one small side thread talking about Don's "soccer game." Clearly, Don and his associates should receive far more attention.
- Sudden changes in behavior by Don may symbolize a denial effort. For example, if Don had previously discussed his hatred for Western civilization frequently in terrorist chat rooms and then disappeared from the chat room, Don's disappearance would qualify as unusual behavior worth investigating.
- Much has been made of terrorist organizations' use of extreme measures to avoid electronic communications that can be directly detected or traced by signals intelligence agencies. However, these extreme measures themselves usually create signals that can be detected. For example, al Qaeda has routinely been cited as using cell phones and email devices only briefly before

discarding them; detectors can be set to look for people who are routinely purchasing and discarding expensive cell phones and pagers, or who are carrying large numbers of electronic devices.[2] Prior to the hotel bombing in Kenya, for instance, observers saw an SUV with ten cell phones and pagers attached to the dashboard—highly unusual behavior that should have been picked up.[3] Similarly, al Qaeda has been cited as using donkeys and motorcycles to carry messages between leaders;[4] detectors can be set to look for people known to have access to expensive vehicles (SUVs, expensive cars) who are suddenly riding donkeys or motorcycles.

Thus, the intentional denial and deception profiles can be used in two ways. The first is to lower the significance of information that would ordinarily be thought of as important but can be put into context of being part of a deception effort. As noted above, information marked as being "deceptive" would be collected separately and reviewed by agents and analysts to look for trends in deception efforts (as well as checked to make sure the information really is deceptive rather than genuine), but it would avoid bogging down the main analytic processes. The second is to raise the significance of information that would ordinarily be ignored but that can be put into context as part of a denial effort to "hide something." Information marked as "indicating denial" would be treated as worth further investigation.

---

[2] See, for example, "One Year On: The Hunt for al-Qaida," *The Guardian*, September 5, 2002, p. 6; and John Diamond, "Terror Group's Messengers Steer Clear of NSA Ears," *USA Today*, October 18, 2002, p. A12.

[3] See, for example, Laurie Goering, "I Shook Hands With Fire: Kenyan Farmer Talked to Bomber Minutes Before They Blew Up Hotel," *Chicago Tribune*, December 2, 2002, p. 1.

[4] See, for example, Michael Elliot, "How Al-Qaeda Got Back on the Attack," *Time*, October 20, 2002.

High-Dimensionality Detection Agents

The detection agents considered up to now have all been fairly simple, rule-following algorithms. It would be desirable to supplement these agents with sophisticated statistical algorithms that find investigation-worthy datasets based on simultaneously considering a large number of fields about those datasets. These algorithms generally involve training a complex classifier (such as a neural network) on instances of investigation-worthy behavior and instances of normal behavior, including observations that initially seemed suspicious but ended up being routine. The result could be a classifier that can detect truly out-of-the-ordinary datasets using rules based on combining complex interactions among data fields—interactions too complicated for a human analyst to develop.[5] (One complication with these algorithms, however, is how we can make their rules context-dependent when they cannot be understood easily. One approach might be to dynamically retrain the algorithms as new data come in, emphasizing the importance of contextually important information while reducing the importance of older observations.) We believe that both these complex algorithms and the simpler, rule-based algorithms have a valuable place in ASAP.

---

[5] DARPA's Wargaming the Asymmetric Environment (WAE) program, for example, is developing complex models to predict the behavior of terrorist groups and individual terrorists. See DARPA Information Awareness Office (2003d).

CHAPTER FIVE

Connecting the Dots

This chapter considers techniques for identifying links between the dots and other, related data previously overlooked. Figure 5.1 shows the area of the ASAP schema on which the chapter focuses—the discovery of relationships that provide additional context to the dots.

Connecting the dots is the purview of *linking agents* in the ASAP architecture. The linking agents would find two types of connections: *similarity connections* and *complementary connections*.

Similarity Connections

Similarity connections link information elements that describe multiple occurrences of identical (or nearly identical) phenomena. In Figure 5.2, the fact that the three people are each helping to plan the same attack is an example of a similarity relationship.

In the prologue, the appearance of new tuna boats in several harbors is another example of a similarity relationship. In threat analysis, similarity connections are primarily signal boosters indicating that certain information (i.e., the tuna boats) should take on more importance to analysts. They tend to be particularly relevant to non-indicative patterns because duplication of the same out-of-the-ordinary event implies that those events are not random occurrences.

Figure 5.1
Finding Relationships Between the Dots

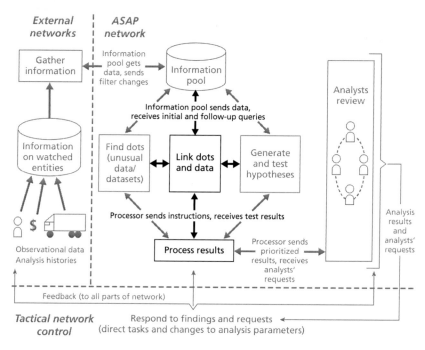

RAND*MG126-5.1*

Figure 5.2
An Example Similarity Relationship

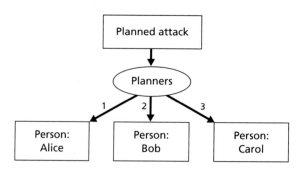

RAND*MG126-5.2*

To search for similarity connections, one looks for observations having features similar to those of an out-of-the-ordinary event. In the tuna scenario in Appendix A, an analyst might note that the sudden surge of tuna boat activity—without a commensurate increase in demand for tuna—is outside standard behavior. A second-order relationship agent (initially described in Chapter Three) would search other databases for similar observations pertaining to unexplained surges in any of the following:

- business activities claiming to be related to tuna catching, processing, or shipping
- tuna boat traffic
- shipping traffic seemingly unrelated to demand
- creation of port-side commercial organizations whose purpose is different from businesses typically found in the harbor, especially if the businesses seem unrelated to any demand in the area.

The technical aspects of searching are straightforward; deciding what constitutes "similar" often is not. Analysts will need to be creative in deriving similarity relationships. In the above example, we created similarity relationships by looking at both the topic of the unusual behavior (tuna, and more generally, international shipping) and the nature of the unusual behavior (significant commercial activity lacking any demand justification).

For finer-grain behavior, one can look for repeated trends in observations. A common example from the intelligence community is that major increases in *chatter* (number of communications sessions) between different groups of a terrorist organization presage a major attack.[1] Here, a second-order relationship agent would search for similar increases in chatter in other parts of the world.

---

[1] See, for example, Dan Eggen and Glenn Kessler, "Signs of Terror Said to Increase; Officials Say Tape, 'Chatter' Indicate Plans for Attacks," *Washington Post*, November 14, 2002, p. A1. The sudden drop-off of chatter can also indicate a pending attack. See, for example, James Risen, "US Increased Alert on Evidence Qaeda Was Planning Two Attacks," *New York Times*, February 14, 2003.

Complementary Connections

Complementary connections link information elements that describe different aspects of a single, larger phenomenon (or potential phenomenon). In Figure 5.3, two of the "attack participants" have been linked with owning a weapon—in this case, a car bomb. The linking of people with an attack mechanism is an example of a complementary connection.

In the scenario in the prologue (see also Appendix A), we discover that some of the tuna boat captains were linked to countries with terrorist enclaves; this is an example of a complementary relationship, as is the discovery that the tuna boat captains' corporate relationships have nothing to do with fishing, forestry, or furniture manufacturing.

Figure 5.3
An Example Complementary Relationship

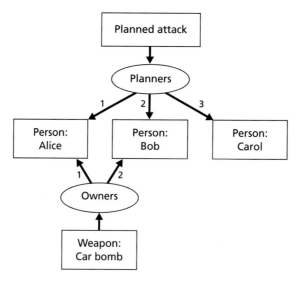

RAND*MG126-5.3*

In threat analysis, complementary connections primarily provide detail—fleshing out the importance of information previously flagged as significant. Similarity connections help indicate which "who, what, when, and where" are significant; the complementary connections help provide the "why and how" of their significance, as well as how the "who, what, when, and where" fit together into a coherent story.

First-order complementary connections, in which one entity is directly linked to another entity through a single piece of data (e.g., Alice owning a particular car) are comparatively easy to find. As an observation enters the network a tracking tool might scan the observation's fields, looking for anything matching fields already associated with data objects. For example, suppose Alice's car is input to the system as being an "unusual vehicle"; scanning the car's registration would create a link from the unusual vehicle observation to both Alice and her car.

Indeed, besides identifying relationships between dots, first-order relationship agents have a more fundamental role in the ASAP architecture. They link incoming observations to all applicable entities (and their data objects), which allows the application of the contextual rules described in Chapter Four.

To make more-sophisticated inferences, one needs to identify *second-order* complementary connections. These connections describe how a sequence of links identifies a previously hidden relationship between two entities. For example, one might identify the fact that Don funds Bob's terror-related activities by tracking Don leaving funds in a particular bank account, the bank account being accessed by Alice and funds being transferred to a second savings account (Carol's), which in turn makes payments to a corporation known to be a shell company for Bob's activities.

We expect that recognizing second-order connections would be a result of automated and human analysis, with computers sifting large databases to create the simpler connections and people piecing together more-detailed relationships when given a set of linked data resulting from their queries. The key for system designers would be to assign relationship-building tasks that leverage people and machines appropriately, playing to their unique strengths.

CHAPTER SIX

Understanding the Dots: Generating and Testing Hypotheses

This chapter considers techniques for understanding the significance of the connected dots by generating and testing hypotheses about them. Figure 6.1 shows the area of the ASAP schema on which the chapter focuses—the discovery of relationships that provide additional context to the dots.

Generating Hypotheses

Once dots have been identified and linked, the next step is to come up with some indication of the significance of the linked dots. This would be done via hypothesis agents that match the dots to *patterns;* dots matching the pattern are a *pattern instance.* In the context of this monograph, we define pattern and pattern instance as follows:

> A *pattern* is a test to determine whether a linked dataset meets certain criteria; datasets meeting the criteria are *pattern instances* and are labeled as having a certain meaning for analysts. In particular, the existence of a pattern instance gives rise either to an indication of potential behavior (increase in certainty) or to the discounting of previously hypothesized behavior (increase in uncertainty).

Figure 6.1
Generating and Testing Hypotheses About the Dots

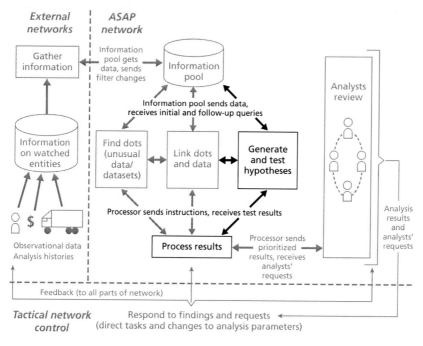

RAND*MG126-6.1*

Within databases, a pattern comprises a set of technical rules defining both the test and what ranges of data are to be tested. Similarly, a pattern instance is defined as a data object pointing to a linked dataset meeting a pattern's criteria.

Although most patterns involve sets having multiple data elements, the following discussion can also be applied to individual signals or values that might be considered as a "pattern of one." For example, a single monetary transfer by someone on the watched list that exceeds a value limit might be sufficient to trigger a potential match. (Single-data-element recognition and triggering are implied whenever patterns are discussed and will not be noted separately.)

Below, we discuss a variety of types of patterns and give example patterns and pattern instances. At the end of this section, we provide a detailed list of the fields and rules comprising a pattern. Note that the examples below are somewhat simplistic and for the most part show straightforward pattern matches. In practice, pattern matching is a complex and active field of research, especially on the messy, incomplete, and uncertain data that would face real-world ASAP systems. In particular, although it might be easy to declare a straightforward "match" in theory, in reality one must make do with partial matches. How to calculate partial matches and what levels of partial warrant analysts' attention in different situations are important questions for research.

A First Pattern-Characterizing Dimension: Indicative and Non-Indicative Patterns

Patterns can be characterized along several different dimensions. The first is whether they are *indicative* or *non-indicative.*

Indicative Patterns. An indicative pattern is associated with a determinate hypothesis of current or future behavior. Such a pattern is found by finding data that meet a set of criteria. Figure 6.2 shows a general pattern designed to identify people potentially planning an explosives attack on behalf of a terror organization. Here, the pattern contains a general template describing certain types of data elements and links between those elements, the ranges of data to be tested for each element, and a rule determining what datasets meet the template "sufficiently." The figure also shows a specific instance of data flagged as meeting the pattern; in this case, the key criterion is having a data path that connects a terror organization to an explosives precursor purchase.

Similarly, in the post-9/11 context, we might expect that a pattern indicating a potential aviation-related attack might be "people on any watch list without any previous airline experience attending flight schools to learn how to pilot passenger jets," or even a more general "people on a terrorist watch list attending flight schools."

Indicative patterns offer the power of specificity because they indicate detailed behavior. However, as noted in our earlier discussions of pattern-matching, their specificity is also a weakness. For example, heuristics agents for patterns similar to the 9/11 pattern would

Figure 6.2
An Indicative Pattern and a Corresponding Instance

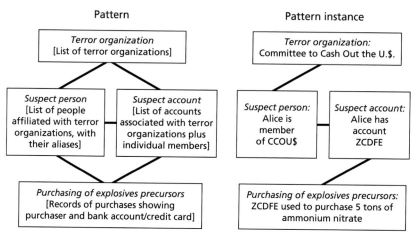

Pattern-matching rule:
One path of connected data from *Terror organization*
to *Purchasing of explosives precursors* is present

RAND*MG126-6.2*

fail to detect people engaged in the majority of other types of terrorist attacks that might involve any large transportation vehicle (air-, ground-, or water-based).

Non-Indicative Patterns. Conversely, a non-indicative pattern is associated with an indeterminate hypothesis of "this behavior is worth investigating further, with some degree of priority." Associated with the *negation* of previous expectations of behavior, these patterns characterize just how unusual the out-of-the-ordinary dots are. While these patterns, by definition, provide much weaker hypotheses than indicative patterns, they do apply to a much wider range of potential threats than indicative patterns do.

Non-indicative pattern instances are found by searching for data violating a set of criteria, where the criteria normally represent a specific status quo in a certain area. Figure 6.3 shows a non-indicative pattern searching for people highly unlikely to be pursuing training as HAZMAT truck drivers; in addition to specifying a match for unusual data, the pattern's rules also define how unusual the data are (here, based on the number of "unlikely" people applying for a HAZMAT training class). The figure also describes a "highly unusual" corresponding instance.

The degree to which such violating data are considered significant depends on how much the data violate the status-quo criteria, with the goal of separating statistical noise from true outliers. Thus, we would be sensitive to multiple entities making the same status-quo violation, for example. The data in Figure 6.3 might be considered especially significant because multiple people from a variety of backgrounds are suddenly taking different jobs.

We would also be sensitive to the same entities engaged in multiple violations of status-quo behavior. In Figure 6.3, should Alice and Bob suddenly close out their bank accounts and book one-way overseas travel to a country recognized as being "unsafe" by the U.S.

Figure 6.3
A Non-Indicative Pattern and a Corresponding Instance

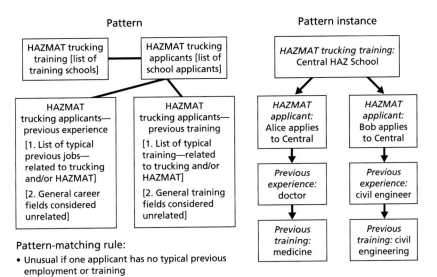

Pattern-matching rule:
• Unusual if one applicant has no typical previous employment or training
• Highly unusual if multiple applications have no typical employment of training plus unrelated career/training

RANDMG126-6.3

State Department, the relative significance of the data would increase even more.

In Chapter Four, we mentioned the development of profiles describing status-quo behavior, actions, and status in different areas. More precisely, hypothesis agents would compare incoming dots with digital representations of the profiles, analyzing deviations to find non-indicative instances.

In general, the analyst would be interested—through additional data collection and analysis—in determining the *meaning* (the specific indicated behavior) of what is initially a non-indicative pattern instance. As noted, reaching detailed conclusions about what a dataset means is the responsibility of the analyst. However, in some cases, it is possible to discover a great deal of meaning through automated techniques. The most common way of doing this is to link an entity in a non-indicative instance to another entity that strongly indicates a particular type of attack. The data in Figure 6.3, for example, contain an initial hint at meaning—HAZMAT operations are directly related to a variety of terrorist attacks. Should Alice be linked directly to a terrorist organization or be overheard describing a truck bombing, the meaning of the data in the figure would be refined further. An ASAP system, then, would have indicative and non-indicative hypothesis agents working in concert; non-indicative agents would flag "worth investigating" datasets, and indicative agents would scour those datasets for potential matches with indicative patterns.

A Second Pattern-Characterizing Dimension: Tests on Data, Metadata, and Reports

At the beginning of Chapter Three, we noted that the ASAP architecture works at three separate levels: review of observational data, review of analysts' behavior with respect to the observational data (what data are queried, what tests are performed, etc.), and review of analysts' reports about the data. Patterns can next be characterized with regard to these levels. Consequently, we have data patterns, metadata patterns, and report patterns.

Data Patterns. These patterns are tested directly against the collected, elemental data traces. The indicative and non-indicative patterns in the previous section were all data patterns.

Metadata Patterns. These patterns are tested against the *metadata,* or data about data, of the collected data. Metadata patterns incorporate information on which agency organizations are collecting or analyzing certain types of data, when, and why. The same dichotomy of indicative and non-indicative patterns that applies for regular data also applies for metadata.

Indicative Metadata Patterns. In terms of metadata, an indicative pattern usually seeks to identify two or more groups that are analyzing the same data, or similar sets of data.[1] The fact that two or more groups are looking at similar data implies that the same data have significance on multiple but related fronts, and that by collaborating, the groups looking at the same data will add to their understanding of the data. In terms of the types of agents, we usually rely on relationship agents to detect the similar analyses (since the analyses are "connected" by their similar attributes).

Figure 6.4, for example, shows a pattern instance of two or more agencies studying the same phenomena. Here, Agency 1 and Agency 2 both find out that they have been investigating Alice, but for different reasons; by collaborating, both would discover that Alice has attended a terror group summit (reason for Agency 1's interest in Alice) and is learning HAZMAT trucking (reason for Agency 2's interest in Alice). Such a discovery has great meaning in terms of whether Alice and her associates are planning an attack and what type of attack they might be planning.

Non-Indicative Metadata Patterns. Non-indicative patterns identify sudden changes in the types of information an agency or agency group is studying. A sudden change in analysis patterns

---

[1] Entities are *similar* if they share a subset of identical attributes. In the tuna boat example, the various boat captains are similar since they are all piloting tuna boats that do not carry tuna.

Figure 6.4
An Instance of Two Agencies Analyzing the Same Data

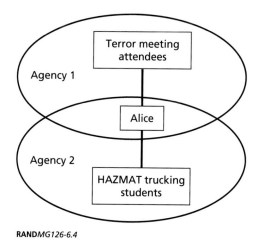

RAND*MG126-6.4*

implies that the agency has learned something or has found something sufficiently unusual to be worth sharing with the wider
antiterrorism community.

In Figure 6.5, for example, Agency 1 has suddenly begun examining records of people who have recently taken HAZMAT
trucking courses; on further investigation, Agency 1 would reveal that
it had the Alice-Bob dataset shown previously.

As another example, in the post 9/11 context, the FBI usually
does not examine students at flight schools and passenger-jet training
centers; it might have been useful if the fact that FBI field offices were
examining such students had been reported to the antiterrorism
community.

Finally, metadata used in analysis would not be restricted to the
types of data in the above examples. Metadata could also be related to
the same analyst and how he is searching and probing; an analyst
spending a great deal of time trying to search for something or find
information about someone can be a useful clue. Metadata can incorporate the number of times a piece of information is used, not necessarily what it was used for. The analyst is frequently interested in the

Figure 6.5
An Instance of an Agency Making Out-of-the-Ordinary Data Requests

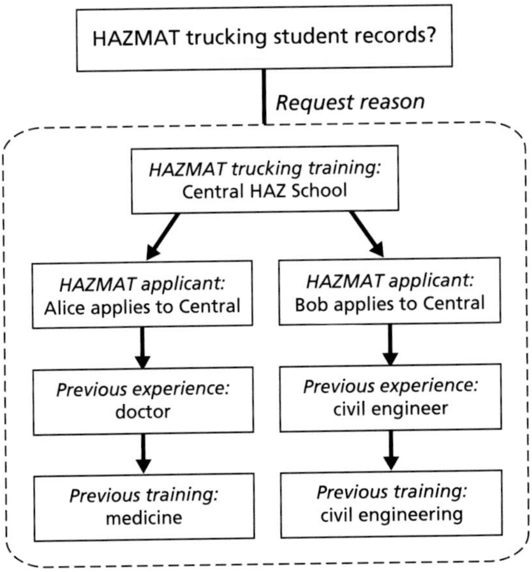

RAND*MG126-6.5*

amount and destinations of email traffic out of a specific IP server rather than the specifics of that traffic.

Report Patterns. These patterns are tested against analysts' reports and notes about the data. These special types of patterns are designed to flag analysts' reports that might otherwise go unnoticed because of organizational and process issues restricting which reports are distributed and acted upon. (This capability is especially important given that, in this case, our description of *analyst* is very broad: Analysts are homeland security professionals who write reports about what they are observing, whether they are official "counterterrorism analysts" or agents doing investigations in the field.) The same dichotomy of indicative and non-indicative patterns applies to data report patterns.

As discussed in Chapter Three, we do not assume that an ASAP system will have the ability to interpret the reports and notes of the analysts. Thus, the patterns discussed below are based primarily on identifying key words and phrases within the reviewed reports.

Indicative Report Patterns. For report patterns, indicative patterns look for key words that indicate an analyst has discovered a signal that directly suggests a particular type of planned attack or other terrorist activity. For example, suppose U.S. Customs agents discover an out-of-the-ordinary shipment of chemicals and write a report identifying the chemicals discovered. An indicative data report agent might scan that report, looking to see if any of those chemicals were explosives or chemical weapons precursors. Other agents might look for reports of discovered guns or knives, and so on.

Non-Indicative Report Patterns. For report patterns, non-indicative results patterns look for key words that indicate that the analyst believes something is out of the ordinary and should be investigated further. For example, one might look for key phrases such as "very unusual," "don't like this at all," "three alarm fire," "disaster waiting to happen." Similarly, we can also look for key phrases that indicate something is probably ordinary and should not be pursued further, such as "a waste of time" or "why are we still doing this."

For both types of patterns, one can analyze trends in the reports as well as individual messages. For example, increases in particular types of key phrases might indicate a general state of heightened suspicions (for non-indicative patterns) or increasing suspicions concerning a particular means of attack (for indicative patterns).

Representation of Patterns

To a computer, patterns of all types and categories share certain key fields and functions. These include

- pattern label/identification
- general type of pattern from which the particular pattern is derived
- a set of sub-elements, with each element representing a life-cycle phase of the pattern
- mathematical rules to determine whether a dataset and its constituent data elements match or violate the particular sub-elements of the pattern

- mathematical rules to assess the results of data analyses, to determine whether to strengthen or weaken belief in the pattern as a whole
- mathematical rules to assess the results of data analyses, to determine when to support transitioning from the current pattern phase to a new phase
- links to all data associated with the pattern (including metadata), plus a history of all analyses performed using the pattern.

The representation of a tested pattern to a human would include all of the above fields and rules (although perhaps not mathematically detailed), plus a set of annotations for each field describing the "story" behind the pattern. The story—written in narrative form—is especially important to human analysts, to help them make sense of the current situation, in terms of what the purpose of the tested pattern is and what they should be doing in response.

High-Dimensionality Pattern Analysis

The patterns considered above are all fairly simple, human-interpretable templates. Much as we augmented the rule-based detection agents with complex statistical detection agents, it would be desirable to supplement these simple patterns with classifiers resulting from sophisticated statistical analysis (again, likely a neural network). These classifiers would result from training on datasets associated not just with "worth investigation" or "not worth investigation" but with characteristics describing different kind of asymmetric attacks or terrorist operations. The result could be a classifier capable of generating valid hypotheses from data whose meaning is unclear to human analysts. We believe that both these complex classifiers and the simpler, human-interpretable templates have an important place in ASAP.

Testing Hypotheses

Pattern instances—and the hypotheses we associate with them—are subject to great uncertainty, which must be recognized and addressed explicitly. The costs of not doing so can be quite high. Consider, for instance, the "Beltway sniper" case. Until the day the shooting suspects were caught, authorities and the media were searching for a white commercial vehicle—either a white box truck, a white van with ladder racks, or a white minivan with ladder racks. This led to widespread dragnets of white commercial vehicles, all of which failed to produce arrests. Still, the *hypothesis* that the snipers were driving a white commercial vehicle was treated as fact. The suspects were finally apprehended driving a dark blue Chevrolet Caprice—on the basis of information entirely unrelated to witness vehicle reports.[2]

It would have been more productive to treat the white commercial vehicle hypothesis explicitly as a hypothesis. In doing so, analysts would have stated the hypothesis, as well as the evidence for it (eyewitness reports from a distance; vehicle drivers at shooting scenes usually did not come forward to dispute claims that they were the snipers) and evidence against it (no eyewitness saw shooters in the vehicle; white commercial vehicles are more noticeable than cars, so the possibility for mistaking where a shot came from is pronounced, especially after people started looking for white vehicles; eyewitnesses reported multiple kinds of white vehicles). Analysts would also have developed tests that would help confirm or disconfirm the hypothesis (continued failure to find suspects in a white vehicle should have helped disconfirm the hypothesis). Finally, they would have identified alternative hypotheses (in this case, a dark-colored Chevrolet Caprice was an alternative hypothesis because one had been reported leaving a D.C. shooting scene[3]). A similar set of tests could have been applied to each alternative hypothesis as well (the Chevrolet Caprice's license plate was scanned ten times during the shooting spree; although details of where the Caprice was scanned have not been made

---

[2] See, for example, Meserve et al., "Two Arrested in Sniper Case," CNN.com, October 24, 2002.

[3] Ibid.

public, repeated scannings at checkpoints near crime scenes should have raised suspicions[4]).

From the above discussion, we can generalize about how to handle uncertainty in hypotheses associated with pattern instances. We explicitly declare the hypothesis associated with each instance ("people in this group are worth further investigation" for non-indicative instances, for example) and some overall rating of the likelihood of the hypothesis. This rating does not need to be quantitative; one can use, for example, Neustadt and May's classic framework (1988) of classifying hypotheses as Known, Presumed, and Unknown. The hypothesis is then associated with evidence for and against it, as well as a list of tests that will confirm or disconfirm it. Once these tests have been identified, the ASAP system is modified to look for observations required by the tests (using contextual rules). Then, as observations are found, the system explicitly revises its likelihood for the hypothesis based on confirming or disconfirming information. Finally, the hypothesis is associated with alternative hypotheses, so that as information comes in, the alternatives are proportionately strengthened or weakened.

Expected-Results Patterns. The tests identified above are implemented with the assistance of expected-results patterns. This class of patterns applies to the results of data analyses, metadata analyses, and reports analyses over time. They test whether, over time, observations of entities classified as being part of a pattern instance confirm or disconfirm the hypotheses associated with that instance. For example, we might expect that people identified as high risk for participating in terrorist activities will participate in those activities (or at least activities that raise additional suspicion). In Figure 6.6, Alice, who has been classified as high risk because she attended a terrorist group meeting and is learning HAZMAT trucking, validates this hypothesis by buying black market plastic explosives.

---

[4] See, for example, Stephen Braun and Mark Fineman, "Sniper Suspects Slipped Past Authorities Time and Again," *Los Angeles Times*, p. A1, November 30, 2002.

Figure 6.6
Validating a Hypothesis

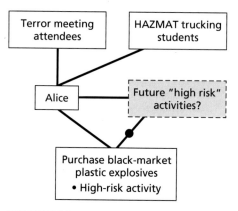

RAND*MG126-6.6*

This methodology would have been of use in the Beltway sniper case. It would have noted the stream of negative findings resulting from days of searching for white commercial vehicles, and weakened the corresponding hypothesis considerably. This weakening would have allowed alternate hypotheses (in the case of the sniper, reports of a dark-colored Chevrolet Caprice with lights turned off) to emerge.

In terms of types of agents, we use heuristics rule agents to detect whether small sets of data elements confirm or disconfirm hypotheses. For large streams of data, trend agents are appropriate.

Beyond strengthening or weakening particular hypotheses, the goal of using expected-results analyses is to improve the range and accuracy of threat assessment over time. We use *indicative expected-results patterns* to determine whether people and activities classified as being high risk really are high risk. Conversely, we use *non-indicative expected-results patterns* to determine whether people and activities characterized as status quo remain "ordinary."

CHAPTER SEVEN

Conclusion

Summary

In this monograph, we have specified a conceptual architecture that identifies, links, and attempts to make useful sense from out-of-the-ordinary information potentially related to terrorist activities. We have specified the major elements and processes of the architecture and discussed the major techniques that would be used to carry out its functions. We believe several features of this architecture make it a unique contribution toward improving the analysis of intelligence information:

- The overall structure of the architecture specifically models empirical research into how proactive and successful problem solvers connect the dots to detect and mitigate potential threats.
- Much of the architecture focuses on detecting behavior that is out of the ordinary from known status-quo behavior and attempting to place that behavior into a threatening context, rather than the detection of behavior fitting particular predetermined patterns indicating known threats. This results in a hybrid structure in which analysts are largely left to determine the deep meaning of such out-of-the-ordinary behavior. *The power of the proposed hybrid structure, however, is that it can detect threatening activities that are obscured to humans because of large*

volumes of data, large dimensionality within the data, and/or de-fining characteristics that have not been seen before.

- The architecture effectively uses context (in the form of contextual rules) to account for what is already known about particular threats or about particular cases of ordinary behavior.
- Even more broadly, the architecture allows for context-dependent analysis processes, in which the analysis activities performed at each step depend on what has been learned to date.

In this concluding chapter, we present a research plan to further develop the framework. We also present a series of recommendations for action to bring the architecture from concept to reality.

A Research Plan

In Chapter One, we listed a number of near-term improvements that would bring about ASAP architecture–like improvements without implementing the architecture's automated components. As the short-term improvements are implemented, research can begin on the automated portion of ASAP. This portion will be of particular value in assisting analysts in identifying out-of-the-ordinary signals in the enormous volumes of data generated by intelligence and conventional collection systems every day.

There is a growing plethora of smart analytic support tools, many of which could be complementary to ASAP (see Appendix B). Because this is a dynamic tool set, the ASAP development team would have to keep track of ongoing and future developments in relevant technologies, including establishing relationships with potential partners at later stages if warranted.

Specifically, in terms of ASAP development itself, we envision a three-phase effort. The first phase would be to develop a detailed architectural plan for the ASAP system and its constituent control and analysis agents. In this phase, architecture-testing scenarios would be developed. The initial architecture would include the detection and connection logic, as well as virtual machine flow architecture and control logic. The architecture would also provide high-level descriptions of detection, linking, and hypothesis agents in such key areas as direct threat detection, international shipping, and air transportation. The first phase would culminate with a description of how the architecture would address a detailed terror-attack scenario. During this phase and the subsequent one, ASAP team members would evaluate and establish a baseline for the state of the art in technologies—such as those described in Chapter Three—that could be used to complement ASAP or implement parts of it. They would also update and maintain their cognizance over those technologies, adjusting architecture designs accordingly. On the nontechnical side, the ASAP team would describe managerial and organizational guidelines to help incorporate ASAP into the work environment. To ensure the acceptance and success of ASAP, it will be essential to work closely with potential end-users—the analysts, field professionals (as available), and others who would interact with the system.

In the second phase, formal design specifications for the agents (detector, processing, linking, and hypothesis) would be created. These specifications would define the objects, methods, and major algorithms employed by the agents. The duration and effort required to execute this phase would depend on the final architecture and agent design.

In the third phase, a prototype system would be developed that would include simple examples of the above agents. The prototype would demonstrate intercepting data, using contextual rules to detect dots. It would use relationship agents to link the dots and use pattern matching/deviation algorithms to generate and test hypotheses. The prototype would also include the control components needed to achieve dynamic, feedback-based control. This phase would also include the design of test methodologies to validate ASAP's performance based on known scenarios, "before and after" methodologies, and other appropriate case studies. Once the prototype is complete, construction and implementation of a real-world ASAP system could commence, moving the ASAP concept from research to reality. The scale of the third phase would depend on the results of the earlier phases.

Conclusion: Recommendations for Action

Our recommendations for action effectively summarize the near-term improvements and research plan we discussed above. We begin with our near-term recommendations. Note that these recommendations need very low levels of investment—nothing beyond a few engineers, communications monitors, and a commitment to sharing information by the initial users. Those providing support functions should be versed in the domain.

We assume that the organization adopting ASAP would determine the necessary level of organizational support and cooperative mechanisms required to implement any or all of the following recommendations for jump-starting ASAP.

- Identify people who understand status-quo activities, and build a library of standardized, brief descriptions of what the status quo looks like for both watched (potentially threatening) and ordinary activities.
- Distribute the status-quo profiles throughout the relevant homeland security communities of interest.
- Establish online virtual communities allowing intelligence, law enforcement, and homeland security professionals to share insights, using the open and moderated electronic posting boards and organizational tools discussed in Chapter One.
- Begin efforts to create search engines and simple detection agents within those virtual communities. These would be linked with the early stages of agent and algorithm development projects within the research plan, as discussed below.
- Begin efforts to create automated agents employing sophisticated statistical models capable of finding the truly threatening atypical behavior in large volumes of high-dimensionality data.

Our longer-term recommendations relate to the development of the automated portions of the ASAP architecture and correspond to the implementation of the research plan described above.

Once these projects have been launched, planning for an ASAP system implementation project would begin. As discussed in Chapter

One, we suggest beginning with a simple system, using first-generation algorithms, within a pilot community within a particular agency. The system would then grow organically over time—adding additional communities and more powerful agents, algorithms, and tools and capitalizing on the real-world experiences of earlier ASAP systems.

Case Study: "The November 9th Incident"

> "Round up the *Un*usual Suspects"
> *(not) Claude Rains, Casablanca*

This appendix presents a scenario describing the unfortunate November 9th incident. The information flow and actions in the scenario are designed to represent what might actually happen, using the current intelligence community as a base.

The first three parts of the appendix describe the lead-up to the sad affair. The first part presents a series of vignettes describing who sees what, who knows what, when they know it, and what they do with the information in the days before the incident. The second part of the appendix presents a "cleaned-up" version of the events leading up to the incident. The third part describes a hypothetical media and government post-mortem of the incident, which provides detailed listings of who knew what pieces of information when, as well as the key findings of a congressional committee report on the sad affair.

The fourth and fifth parts of this appendix describe how an ASAP system might have helped connect the dots prior to November 9th. The fourth part describes the information ASAP agents would have detected and flagged as being out of the ordinary; the fifth part describes how analysts would have interacted with the system.

Version 1—Initial Case Study of the November 9th Incident

[October 12, 2002] As soon as he heard the news about the bombing in Bali, the Singapore desk analyst at CIA Headquarters near Washington, D.C., Fred "Woody" Johnson, was shocked—it was practically in his backyard (analytically speaking). Given that, he put himself and colleagues on "heightened alert" for any behaviors, events, or activities that would fit "classic" terrorist patterns now identified after September 11, 2001. He also set his current suite of analytical tools to comb more finely through the data he received, looking for indicators of potential terrorist activity (transportation of chemicals or explosives, sightings of known or suspected terrorist individuals, etc.)

In the course of reviewing every piece of official, special, and open-source reporting from the region since the event, Johnson found nothing more interesting beyond reports of two Arabs hauled in for false driver's licenses and an unattended duffel bag containing hockey equipment and a strange odor at the airport. Nothing highly unusual came across his "radar screen," and Johnson soon convinced himself that everything was "business as usual" on his watch.

The two unrelated driver's license incidents were reported in a weekly "incident summary" (week of Sept. 23–29) that the local U.S. Embassy got from local police. The students involved had been pulled over at the Singapore International Airport for driving too slowly in front of the Saudi Air terminal but never stopping—just continually driving past. This was unusual, but the officer figured they just didn't understand how the airport was laid out and were trying to meet someone. These reports actually predated the Bali bombing by two weeks, having taken their sweet time to filter their way through the "ROUTINE" cable channels and make it to Johnson's inbox. The day following the bombing, the airport security sweep team had seen the large, heavy, awkward, unmarked duffel bag in the passenger waiting lounge of the Saudi Air terminal and brought in their K-9 unit. Dutifully doing their job, the dogs whined at the bag but did not indicate that it contained any explosives or drugs. Johnson noted the incident and smiled when he thought about the dogs finding smelly gym socks. Since it came from an international travel alert for government officials, at least this report had made it to his desk less than 24 hours after the incident occurred.

In early August, the *Tuna Daily* in Seattle announced that its main advertising sponsor, the Seattle Flying Fish Shipbuilders, had delivered the last of a record order for 24 high-speed tuna boats. They had been ordered in February and the customer was rumored to be interested in another large order. Talk at Hal's Burger 'N Beer Barn focused on who would have placed such an order because the locals knew that none of the Seattle fishing operations had done so—nor could even afford to. The paper said only that the boats had been ordered by a "wealthy shipping concern registered out of Panama." The fishermen were bent out of shape at the potential competition. Tuna fishing was a low-margin operation. Their only hope was that U.S. health experts would keep publishing how healthy it was to eat tuna and encourage U.S. and other Western populations to do so.

Since June, an international group of Arab students had been planning the fall Arab Student League Forum for students studying in southwest Asia. These events took place semiannually for Arab students to compare notes on experiences adjusting to living as Arabs in Asian cultures. The event, scheduled for November 11, was to be hosted by the Arab Student League delegation in Hong Kong. Now with the bombing, the group wondered if it was ever going to happen. The planning committee had encountered what it thought were roadblocks from the local Hong Kong authorities every step of the way. Was this discrimination or merely Chinese socialism and bureaucracy at their finest?

In planning the program, the group handed out a survey—with predictable responses. While racial profiling was nowhere near the hot topic it would have been in Western countries, the students all mentioned an uneasy feeling of "awareness" and many commented they were singled out for things such as extra questioning, ID checks, and approvals for routine student activities. During the planning session on October 20, Harim Mujen, the delegate from Kuala Lumpur, even commented, "Yeah, my parents can't stand the way I'm singled out here. They think it's because they're so wealthy and I might be a target for kidnapping. I think it's just the opposite. I'm starting to get fed up with this place. I want to be somewhere where I really belong and can make a difference for something I believe in—like back home in Syria." The group came to no consensus, per se, but there was an unmistakable empathy and bond that grew stronger among them. They all agreed to stay in touch regularly by email.

At their monthly International Business Symposium on Friday, October 18, U.S. and British Embassy officials were talking with local executives from one of the large commercial shipping firms in the Singapore harbor. One executive commented to host State Department colleague Karen Scott, "I can't understand why this new company moved in and immediately placed an order for slips for 18 tuna-fishing boats. These guys should understand there isn't much market for tuna processing here. We run a high-class harbour and space is at an incredible premium. Besides, they're going to totally disrupt our well-managed schedule by adding all these new departures and arrivals. I hope they won't last long. These guys think since they have connections, they can do anything." Scott noted this would fill out the remainder of her weekly report and went from the meeting to a "wine and dine" weekend event with her beau. Early the following week she sent a ROUTINE cable from her desk back at the Commerce Section to law enforcement, drug enforcement, maritime, and intelligence agencies. She included State Department Headquarters as well as field offices on the distribution.

Later that week, on October 22, a small advertisement in the classified section of the *Singapore Times* offered: "Union wages, overtime, full benefits, and immediate employment. Paid in cash daily," for the first 100 laborers to apply for loading and unloading ships in the harbor. The economics officer at the embassy in Singapore noted the ad because there had been growing unemployment among blue-collar workers in the city and crime had been rising. He hoped this might be the indicator that things were turning around economically for this important port city. After sending an email to Scott, the commercial attaché, he fired off a "Good news on the employment front" cable to the State Department and Department of Commerce back in D.C. Many of the workers applying for these jobs were not

Singapore citizens, so he sent copies to appropriate desk officers in the State Department for the countries that had the highest population of migrant workers in Singapore—mainly Malaysia and other Pacific Rim countries. He sent a ROUTINE copy to members of the intelligence community with branches concerned with employment, migration, and population trends, including Intelligence and Research at the State Department. Since 9/11, he had been told to be extra diligent in reporting any hiring oddities, but he figured no one would ever see the cable anyway. If every other officer was doing what he was doing, there must be a big pile of cables back home. At least he did what he was supposed to do, so he was covered.

It was October 4 before the local magistrate, Mr. Peekuj, got around to reviewing the last month's [September's] applications for local permits, licenses, and other official approvals. Peekuj was frustrated by a new tuna importer's "RUSH-Priority" application for licenses for 18 tuna boats, as well as for immediate approval to exceed normal weight and cargo limits. It appeared that the applications had been filed in early September—almost a month ago. He'd never heard of the company making the request, but then he tried not to pay a lot of attention to maritime matters. The boats were registered in Panama. Well, nothing terribly unusual about that. Everyone knew how easy ship registry was there—and cheap too.

Peekuj was so irritated by this request that he stuffed it into the bottom of his inbox and told his deputy, Mr. Nawram, "Go find out who these guys are." Nawram, who was also a recruited asset of the local CIA station, called his case officer, Randy May, to explain he could not make a routine meeting "because I've gotta go find out what these idiots are doing with 18 tuna boats in our high-class commercial harbour and why they're already fussing they don't have arrangements for immediate docking and sailing. These clowns don't have any of the appropriate paperwork on file." The CIA officer noted the peculiarity and included it in his weekly report to headquarters, including the specific Singapore desk officers at CIA (Woody Johnson), State, and DEA, among others. At least he had something to cable back this week.

At the end of September, the prominent Mujen family of Damascus announced they would be closing their business and taking an extended holiday in the Far East to visit family abroad, review some recent investments, and look for other acquisition opportunities. In Kuala Lumpur, Harim Mujen was delighted to learn that his family would be arriving within ten days to see him. He couldn't wait to tell them what life was like as an Arab student in the Far East. Their telex said they'd be visiting Singapore and Thailand en route as well. What did he care; he just wanted them to take him home. This was his chance to make his case for returning to "his part of the world." Perhaps he could convince them to let him finish his studies in Saudi Arabia.

The week of October 28 was one of the high points of the year for various U.S., British, and other Western diplomats as official representatives met for a regional conference in Sydney hosted by the director of the Australian diplomatic corps, Timothy Smythe. The respective intelligence and law enforcement services from the region were invited as appropriate. Most viewed these events either as a great excuse to get out of the office and have some R&R or as a colossal waste of time, filled with useless meetings and not enough real work done to take advantage of having such a group assembled. However, this week's meeting included the American holiday Halloween and everyone was looking forward to the various high jinks. You never knew who was joking and who was serious, even among close friends.

During the opening cocktail hour, Smythe commented to Tynes, Lupin, and Arden, who was just finishing a round-the-world tour of new FBI stations overseas, "You guys sure have it easy, I just got stuck down here trying to figure out why the number of tuna boats coming in and out of here has doubled in August and none appears to be permanently based here. Twenty-four of them. Seems most of them showed up over two weeks in mid-to-late August. That's a large fleet. They look new, but almost every one is requesting complete paint jobs and won't let local contractors do the work. They're using immigrant labor only. We just wish they'd quit tying up the slips and bring some long-term business to the area. They don't even seem to have much fishing gear on board. What are these guys, fools? Not clear if they know tuna from sardines. Gossip is that a spoiled rich kid with oil money is backing it and has some family connections in other shipping concerns. Hope they give him some pointers." The CIA chief of station, Mark Lupin, commented, "Gosh, one of my officers mentioned some hassle with a tuna operation back in Singapore. I thought he was just complaining as usual." Lupin decided to send a report noting this coincidence when he returned to the office on November 4.

Given the recent anniversary of September 11 and vague threats reported by the FBI and CIA, the Coast Guard had been maintaining a heightened vigilance with respect to ports along the east coast of the United States, especially those doing large commercial shipping. During their weekly review with the Maryland Port Authority and related services on October 14, the Department of Commerce representative commented, "This October 1st request bothers me. Why are we getting Panamanian tuna boats requesting docks and berths in Baltimore, and didn't a tuna boat company just lease a wharf in Philadelphia? Normally they go farther south. We haven't seen any increased orders from tuna processors locally and no one seems to be forecasting an increase on such short notice—just the opposite. The boats seem to be coming from southwest Asia or the Pacific Rim, but we're not sure. When we talked to some of the captains on the 11th, the only story we could get from them was that they were using tuna boats to carry teak wood to furniture builders in North Carolina and up the coast. They said they had railroad connections from here on south." A few lines about this were included in the weekly summary that was submitted October 16.

The October 23 DEA staff meeting at least had some life in its agenda. DEA officials in Florida noted the October 16 report with interest at their regular staff meeting because the last two raids they had conducted on suspected drug runners resulted in capturing modified tuna boats. But, upon further inspection, DEA had to release the boats that had requested berths in Baltimore because nothing more than heavy, odd-shaped containers and funny smells could be found on the boats. The captains, who spoke little English, were clearly annoyed and got on their radios quickly to others in their fleet.

The next morning, anxious to make a good impression and demonstrate her irreplaceable value, Susan Mandetti woke the DEA chief of operations at the Key West base before his first cup of coffee. She'd just received her CIA copy of Karen Scott's report from the embassy in Singapore and could barely sit still: Could there be a connection between these two sets of east coast tuna boats and the ones in Scott's report? Being a CIA officer on detail to another agency sure had its advantages. Maybe her quick eye and quick thinking would get her promoted.

Back at CIA Headquarters, Woody Johnson called an October 25 meeting with his regional specialist colleagues from around the Beltway. His opening comment to this interagency task force was, "I sure thought we'd see a lot more unusual activity in the region after the Bali bombing. I'm worried we're missing something. There are so many vulnerable targets. I did see several cables about a new 'Arab-American Friendship League' starting, as well as a new mosque opening later this fall. I wonder if these are not fronts for other activities and why is the mosque advertising so many social events for young people?" Two colleagues agreed with him and also added, "We've noticed an increase in Arab graduate students leaving their universities early and returning home. That seems odd because these are usually wealthy families with no financial worries about education and the tradition is to return with a completed graduate degree and become a valuable member of a profession. Let's get INS involved and see if anything similar is happening in the U.S."

Several phone calls and emails later, the counterterrorism representative for INS, Sam Trowl, said he had a few minutes for his colleagues' "concerns." He invited his protégé, Bill Sands, to join him for the conference call. After hearing their observation and "suspicions" he sheepishly replied, "We still don't know who is actually in the country studying or if they are at the university they said they were attending when their visa was granted, so unless it's a visa/immigration violation, we're not getting involved." Bill was not completely satisfied with this but didn't want to say anything in front of his boss, so he politely said, "I'll get back to you guys if I see anything that will help you."

In the Friday Business Section of the Seattle *Daily Post,* the Chamber of Commerce announced it would be holding a special reception for the new Syrian owner of the Seattle Flying Fish Shipbuilders, who was arriving the following Tuesday, November 5, from Kuala Lumpur. From an economic point of view, the Panamanian tuna boat order earlier in the year had helped make a dent in unemployment locally, so the chamber wanted to congratulate the Mujen family on the growth in their business. Of course, the chamber hoped this wealthy Syrian family would be a source of other investments in the Seattle maritime industry.

Although the embassy in Singapore was the scene of "childish infighting" and the usual Monday-morning quarterbacking—not all that uncommon in U.S. diplomatic facilities abroad—this was ridiculous. During a "staff meeting," Karen Scott had seen the Chamber of Commerce announcement while scanning Seattle news headlines online and said, "Hmmm. There can't be too many new tuna boats being built at any one point in time. I wonder if the new tuna fishing boats in our harbor were built in Seattle? That would be odd—most local boats are built in Korea or Taiwan."

At that point, Randy May interrupted and said, "Since when are you interested in the local tuna trade? I wish somebody had told me about this, I have some 'inside' reporting that might be related. Why am I always out of the loop?" Not wanting any more turf battles and wanting to "cooperate and coordinate" appropriately, Tynes looked at Lupin and said "Mark, get these kids playing nicely in the sandbox, OK? I don't want to hear any more of this crap," and walked out puffing on his pipe. Lupin glared at Scott and May. The two of them understood very clearly they should be coordinating closely on this Friday's "joint" report. Maybe Karen had more on the ball than May suspected and wasn't just a socialite. He'd pay closer attention to her in the future as well. She might know some interesting and useful folks. He still sent out his own private CIA channel cable that afternoon.

By early November, the U.S. Coast Guard and Maryland Port Authority had decided they were tired of these rogue tuna boat captains' behavior. Doing a little homework, they checked to see if there *no*

no had been a ~~dramatic increase in local buyers' demand for tuna~~, if ~~permits had been granted to import teak from new sources~~—the Far East in particular—and looked under as many rocks as they could think of, but they ~~found only worms for their week's work~~. They did their best to interview the few captains who would spend five minutes with them and gave the captains' names to the FBI, DEA, and INS.

As usual, they sorted through the common "John Smith"–type Arabic names, such as Mustaffah, Amdu, and Mujen, including those on various watch lists. While none of the captains specifically raised any eyebrows, Mujen certainly got around. Further background investigation did show that ~~several of the captains had family connections in Qatar, Yemen, and Syria: None of them were fishing, furniture or forestry related. Two captains' names did match those of foremen working for a firm in Seattle some six months ago—making boats.~~

. . . *On November 9th something very bad happened* . . .

Version 2—Structured in Chronological Order with Background Information Added, Noise Removed

In June, the Arab Student League in Hong Kong started planning for a conference of Arab students studying in southwest Asia, to be held on November 11. Well over a hundred participants were expected. These events take place semiannually and allow the students to discuss issues arising from living as Arabs in Asian cultures. The group encountered some delays in obtaining a city permit for the conference. Harim Mujen was a member of the social committee.

In early August, the *Tuna Daily* in Seattle announced that Seattle Flying Fish Shipbuilders had delivered the last of 24 high-speed tuna boats to a Panamanian customer. They had been ordered in February and were to be ultimately delivered to Singapore.

At the end of September, the prominent Mujen family in Syria announced in the society column of the Damascus paper that they would be taking an extended holiday in the Far East, including Singapore, to visit family before reviewing their recently acquired investments in Seattle and Los Angeles. Harim Mujen made a note to book his travel to Hong Kong via Singapore before October 6 to get the four-week advance booking rate for the conference.

On October 4, the local Singapore magistrate reviewed the September 8 rush application by a Panamanian firm to berth 18 vessels in the harbor. Via an agent, the local CIA officer noted the particulars and included the incident in his weekly report to Headquarters, including the specific Singapore desk officers at CIA, State Department, and DEA. When he heard about the October 12 bombing in Bali, the Singapore desk analyst at CIA Headquarters, Fred "Woody" Johnson, put himself and colleagues on heightened alert for any behavior, event, or activity that would fit classic terrorist patterns now identified after 9/11. In his weekly report, he noted an older report of two Arabs with false driver's licenses and an abandoned bag at the airport.

MO

During an October 14 meeting with State Department and law enforcement agencies, the Coast Guard and others discussed an October 1 request by a Panamanian tuna boat firm for docks and berths in Baltimore and how a dock had recently been leased to a tuna boat company in Philadelphia. The boats were reported to be coming from southwest Asia or the Pacific Rim. The captains claimed that they were using tuna boats to carry teak wood to furniture builders in North Carolina and up the coast. A few lines about this were included in the weekly summary that was submitted on October 16.

At the meeting of international businesses in Singapore on October 18, Karen Scott of the State Department learned about the odd behavior of a tuna boat company in the Singapore harbor. Early the following week, she sent a routine cable from her desk at the Commerce Section to law enforcement, drug enforcement, maritime, and intelligence agencies. On the distribution list, she included main State Department and CIA Headquarters, as well as field offices.

Later that week, on October 23, the economics officer at the Singapore embassy noted hiring increases in the harbor, and, after sending an email to Scott on the Commerce Desk, he fired off a "Good news on the employment front" cable to the State Department and Department of Commerce back in Washington. He also sent copies to appropriate desk officers in the State Department for the countries that had the highest population of migrant workers in Singapore: Malaysia and other Pacific Rim countries. He sent a low-priority paper copy to members of the intelligence community with branches concerned with employment, migration, and population trends.

On October 24, Miami DEA officials noted the October 16 summary report through Susan Mandetti, a CIA officer on detail to the Miami office, who reported to the DEA chief of operations in Key West about the possible relationship to activities in Baltimore and Philadelphia. The report was also sent to various intelligence agencies.

On October 26, Woody Johnson noted to the interagency task force about lower-than-expected terrorist activity after the Bali bombing and how he had seen cables about the start of a new "Arab-American Friendship League" starting and a new mosque opening later that fall. Others also noted an increase in Arab graduate students leaving their universities early and returning to the Middle East. The student movement was odd and the Singapore CIA Desk decided to involve the INS to see if something similar was happening in the United States.

The counterterrorism representative for INS, Sam Trowl, had not noticed anything odd but was probably too buried under his own paperwork to notice.

The week of October 28 marked a yearly regional conference held in Sydney, hosted by the Australian diplomatic corps. The Australian host commented to the U.S. State Department, CIA, and FBI representatives about problems with 24 tuna boats. The CIA chief of station, Mark Lupin, noted that one of his officers had mentioned some hassle with a tuna operation back in Singapore and included this in his November 4 report.

On November 1, the Chamber of Commerce in Seattle, Washington, announced it would have a special reception for the Syrian owner of the Seattle Flying Fish Shipbuilders, who was arriving on November 5 from Kuala Lumpur.

On November 4, Randy May, CIA officer at the U.S. Embassy in Singapore, discovered that Karen Scott had also noted tuna boat activity in Singapore and in the Seattle paper. He noted this in his Friday report.

By November 5, the U.S. Coast Guard and Maryland Port Authority had given the names of the tuna boat captains to the CIA, FBI, DEA, and INS. The FBI, DEA, and INS did not find anything unusual about the tuna boat captains in the first search. None of the captains specifically raised any eyebrows and there was nothing on them directly in the system. Further background investigation did show several of the captains with family connections in Qatar, Yemen, and Syria: None of the families had any connection to fishing, furniture, or forestry. Two of the captains had worked recently for the same firm in Seattle—a boatbuilding concern.

. . . *On November 9th something very bad happened* . . .

Post-Mortem Analysis

In conducting a post-mortem of this sad event, it is important to look at the evidence and review the processes. First, what facts were known and when were they known? We use two sources: overt and investigative reporting and the government's internal review.

By mid-November, the reporters were clamoring for details on who knew what, what was known when, and how the obvious signals could have been missed . . . again. Some investigative reporters had started documenting the events and the timelines before 11/9.

The following information elements existed in the commercial, city, state, and federal records and were disclosed on the evening news by the reporters on November 19. It still wasn't known for sure who was behind the event, but the reporters were sniffing out anything that might be related:

February 4   Twenty-four tuna boats are ordered in Seattle for export to Australia under the Panamanian flag; export papers are filed.

June 13	A Hong Kong city permit is issued for an Arab student conference in November.
August 6	A Seattle paper announces completion of an order for 24 tuna boats to a Panamanian concern.
August 9	Twenty-four Panamanian tuna boats arrive in Sydney, are registered in the harbor.
September 8	An application is made for 18 tuna boat berths in Singapore's harbor by a Panamanian firm.
September 29	The Mujen family announces in the Damascus paper its trip via the Far East to Seattle and Los Angeles to visit recently acquired investments.
September 30	Two Arab students are detained for having false driver's licenses at Singapore airport.
October 6–7	More than 100 Arab students had booked travel to Hong Kong for November 10.
October 1	A Panamanian firm requests off-loading privileges at Baltimore public wharf.
October 10	A wharf in Philadelphia is leased to a Panamanian firm.
October 12	A bombing in Bali is reported on all of the news wires and governmental services. *Small attack?*
October 13	Abandoned luggage is found at the Singapore airport, Saudi Air Terminal.
October 23	Classified ads for high-paying, cash work on the docks appear in Singapore paper.
November 1	Seattle paper reports Chamber of Commerce reception for Mujen family from Syria.

The following information elements were generated by the intelligence process itself and were part of the official record that was uncovered during the internal review after 11/9:

October 4   CIA officer in Singapore reports tuna boats causing problems in the harbor.

October 14   Singapore Desk at CIA Headquarters reviews reports of two Arab students detained September 30 and abandoned luggage found at the Singapore airport.

October 16   Maryland Coast Guard reports Panama-flagged boats acting unconventionally and being uncooperative in Baltimore and possible relationship to tuna boat activity at Philadelphia. MO

October 21   Commerce Section of U.S. Embassy in Singapore reports notable commercial activity by tuna boat company.

October 23   Economics officer at U.S. Embassy in Singapore notes nonroutine hiring practices at the harbor, new tuna boat activity, and potential for economic recovery.

October 24   Miami DEA reports possible relationship between local intercepted tuna boats and activity in Baltimore and Philadelphia.

October 28   Singapore Desk at CIA Headquarters learns of unusual number of Arab students returning home. actg

November 4   CIA Chief of Station in Singapore reports coincidence of problems with tuna boats in Sydney and Singapore.

November 5   Maryland Coast Guard reports the names of five of the tuna boat captains.

November 7   INS, FBI, DEA request reports on background information regarding tuna boat captains.

November 8   CIA officer in Singapore reports commercial, economic, and personal information that the tuna story and the Seattle news article are possibly correlated.

These eleven reports were then distributed as follows:

Behavior

October 4   CIA officer in Singapore reports fishing firm with 18 tuna boats causing administrative problems in the harbor. Distributed to CIA Headquarters Asia Desk, Singapore Desk, Main State Department, DEA.

October 14   Desk Officer at CIA Station, Singapore reports two Arab students detained September 30 and abandoned luggage found in Saudi Air Terminal at the Singapore airport. Distributed to CIA Headquarters Asia Desk, Singapore Section.

October 16   Maryland Coast Guard reports Panama-flagged boats *behavior* acting unusual in Baltimore and possible relationship to tuna boat activity at Philadelphia. Distributed to CIA Headquarters Counter Terrorism Center, FBI, Coast Guard.

October 21   Commerce Section at U.S. Embassy in Singapore reports anomalous commercial activity by tuna boat company. Distributed to CIA Headquarters Asia Desk, Singapore Section, FBI, DEA, Coast Guard.

✻ acqil dist?

October 23   Economics officer at U.S. Embassy in Singapore reports unusual hiring practice at the harbor, new tuna boat activity, and potential for economic recovery. Distributed to Main State Department, Commerce Desk at U.S. Embassy in Singapore, D.C. Dept. of Commerce. Routine priority copies to CIA Headquarters Asia Desk, FBI, DEA, Coast Guard, INS.

October 24   Miami DEA reports possible relationship between intercepted tuna boats and Baltimore–Philadelphia activity. Distributed to CIA Headquarters Counterterrorism Center, FBI, DEA, Coast Guard.

October 28   Singapore Desk at CIA Headquarters hears of unusual number of Arab students returning home. Distributed to INS.

November 4   CIA Chief in Singapore reports coincidence of tuna boat problems and oddities in Sydney and Singapore. Distributed to CIA Headquarters Asia Desk, Singapore Desk, CIA Singapore Station.

November 5   Maryland Coast Guard reports the names of five of the tuna boat captains. Distributed to CIA Headquarters Counter Terrorism Center, FBI, DEA, INS.

November 7   INS, FBI, DEA request reports on background information regarding tuna boat captains. Distributed to CIA Headquarters Counter Terrorism Center, Coast Guard.

November 8   CIA officer in Singapore reports commercial, economic, and personal information that the tuna boats and the Seattle news article are possibly correlated. Distributed to CIA Headquarters Asia Desk, Singapore Desk, CIA Counter Terrorism Center, Main State Department, DEA Headquarters, and field offices.

Interviews with the various agencies and representatives showed that the intelligence community had, through overt means, collected the following information that was also eventually disclosed by the press:

August 9   Twenty-four Panamanian tuna boats arrive in Sydney, are registered in the harbor. Reported November 4 by CIA Chief of Station in Singapore.

September 8   An application is made for 18 berths in Singapore's harbor by a Panamanian firm. Reported October 4 by CIA Officer Randy May in Singapore.

September 30 Two Arab students are detained for having false driver's licenses at Singapore airport. Reported October 14 by CIA Headquarters, Singapore Desk.

October 10   A wharf in Philadelphia is leased to a Panamanian firm. Reported October 14 by U.S. Dept. of Commerce, Coast Guard, Maryland Port Authority.

October 10   A Panamanian firm requests off-loading privileges at Baltimore public wharf. Reported October 14 by U.S. Dept. of Commerce, Coast Guard, Maryland Port Authority.

October 12   Bombing in Bali is reported on all of the news wires and governmental services. Reported October 12 by all agencies.

October 13   Abandoned luggage is found at the Singapore airport, Saudi Air Terminal. Reported October 14 by CIA Station, Singapore Desk Officer.

October 23   Classified ads in Singapore paper for high-paying, cash work on the docks. Reported October 23 by Economics officer at U.S. Embassy, Singapore.

November 1   Seattle paper reports Chamber of Commerce reception for Mujen family from Syria. Reported November 5 by Commerce Desk at U.S. Embassy, Singapore.

So, who knew what, when?

In Singapore

CIA Station

October 4   Since mid-September, a firm owning 18 tuna boats had been causing problems in the harbor.

October 12   The bombing in Bali was reported on all of the news wires and governmental services.

November 4   Coincidence of problems with tuna boats and oddities in Sydney and Singapore; reported by CIA Chief of Station in Singapore.

November 4   By August 9, 24 Panamanian tuna boats had arrived in Sydney, were registered in the harbor; reported by CIA Chief of Station in Singapore.

November 4   Unusual commercial activity by tuna boat company; reported by Commerce Desk, U.S. Embassy.

November 5   Seattle paper reported Chamber of Commerce reception for Mujen family from Syria; reported by Commerce Desk, U.S. Embassy.

U.S. Embassy – Commerce Desk

October 12   Bombing in Bali is reported on all of the news wires and governmental services.

October 18   Odd commercial activity by tuna boat company noted at reception.

November 5   On November 1, Seattle paper reported Chamber of Commerce reception for Mujen family from Syria.

U.S. Embassy – Economics Desk

October 12   Bombing in Bali is reported on all of the news wires and governmental services.

October 21   Odd commercial activity by tuna boat company; reported by Commerce Desk (Scott).

October 23   Classified ads appeared in Singapore paper for high-paying, cash work on the docks.

November 5   Seattle paper reported Chamber of Commerce reception for Mujen family from Syria; reported by Commerce Desk at U.S. Embassy, Singapore.

At CIA Headquarters:

CIA Headquarters, Asia Desk

October 4   Firm owning tuna boats causing problems; reported by CIA officer in Singapore.

October 12   Bombing in Bali is reported on all of the news wires and governmental services.

October 14   Reports of two Arab students detained September 30 and abandoned luggage found at the Singapore airport; received by Singapore Desk at CIA Headquarters.

October 21   Odd commercial activity by tuna boat company; reported by Commerce Section in Singapore.

November 1   Odd hiring practice at the Singapore harbor, new tuna boat activity, and potential for economic recovery; October 23 report from Economics officer in Singapore.

November 4   Coincidence of tuna boat problems and oddities in Sydney and Singapore; reported by CIA Chief in Singapore.

November 8   Commercial, economic, personal information on the tuna boats and the Seattle news article as being possibly correlated; from CIA officer in Singapore.

CIA Headquarters Counter Terrorism Center

October 12   Bombing in Bali is reported on all of the news wires and governmental services.

October 16   Panama-flagged boats acting strangely in Baltimore and possible relationship to tuna boat activity at Philadelphia; reported by Maryland Coast Guard.

October 24   Possible relationship between intercepted tuna boats and Baltimore–Philadelphia activity; reported by Miami DEA.

November 5   The names of five of the tuna boat captains; reported by Maryland Coast Guard.

November 7   Background checks done on the five tuna boat captains.

November 8   Commercial, economic, and officer's own information on the tuna boats and the Seattle news article as being possibly correlated; report from CIA officer in Singapore.

CIA Headquarters Singapore Desk

October 4   Firm owning tuna boats causing problems; from CIA officer in Singapore

October 12   Bombing in Bali is reported on all of the news wires and governmental services

October 14   On October 13, abandoned luggage was found at the Singapore Saudi Air Terminal

October 14   On September 30, two Arab students were detained for having false driver's licenses at Singapore airport.

October 28   Hears of unusual number of Arab students returning home.

November 4   Coincidence of tuna boat headaches and oddities in Sydney and Singapore; from CIA Chief in Singapore.

November 8   Commercial, economic, and personal information on the tuna boats and the Seattle news article are possibly correlated; from CIA officer in Singapore.

At Departments of State and Commerce:

Department of State

October 4   Tuna boats causing problems in the harbor; from CIA officer in Singapore.

October 12   Bombing in Bali is reported on all of the news wires and governmental services.

October 23   Odd hiring practice at the Singapore harbor, new tuna boat activity, and potential for economic recovery; reported by Economics officer at U.S. Embassy in Singapore.

November 8   Commercial, economic, and personal information on the tuna boats and the Seattle news article are possibly correlated; reported by CIA officer in Singapore.

Department of Commerce

October 12   Bombing in Bali is reported on all of the news wires and governmental services.

October 14   On October 10, a wharf in Philadelphia was leased to a Panamanian firm.

October 14   On October 10, a Panamanian firm requested offloading privileges at Baltimore public wharf.

October 23   Odd hiring practice at the Singapore harbor, new tuna boat activity, and potential for economic recovery; reported by Economics officer at U.S. Embassy in Singapore.

At the Coast Guard:

Maryland Coast Guard

October 14   On October 10, a wharf in Philadelphia was leased to a Panamanian firm.

October 14   On October 10, a Panamanian firm requested offloading privileges at Baltimore public wharf.

October 12   Bombing in Bali is reported on all of the news wires and governmental services.

October 16–31 Names of five of the tuna boat captains.

October 21   Odd commercial activity by tuna boat company; reported by Commerce Section, U.S. Embassy in Singapore.

October 24   Possible relationship between intercepted tuna boats and Baltimore–Philadelphia activity; reported by Miami DEA.

November 1   Odd hiring practice at the Singapore harbor, new tuna boat activity, and potential for economic recovery; October 23 report from U.S. Embassy in Singapore.

Florida Coast Guard/DEA Joint Task Force

October 12   Bombing in Bali is reported on all of the news wires and governmental services.

October 16   Panama flagged boats acting strangely in Baltimore and possible relationship to tuna boat activity at Philadelphia; from Maryland Coast Guard.

October 21   Odd commercial activity by boat company; reported by Commerce Section at U.S. Embassy in Singapore.

October 24   Possible relationship between intercepted tuna boats and Baltimore–Philadelphia activity; from Miami DEA.

November 1   Odd hiring practice at the Singapore harbor, new tuna boat activity and potential for economic recovery; October 23 report from U.S. Embassy in Singapore.

Coast Guard Headquarters

October 12   Bombing in Bali is reported on all of the news wires and governmental services.

October 16   Panama-flagged boats acting uncooperatively in Baltimore and possible relationship to tuna boat activity at Philadelphia; from Maryland Coast Guard.

October 21   Odd commercial activity by tuna boat company; from Commerce Section in Singapore.

October 24   Possible relationship between intercepted tuna boats and Baltimore–Philadelphia activity; reported by Miami DEA.

November 1   Odd hiring practice at the Singapore harbor, new tuna boat activity, and potential for economic recovery; October 23 report from U.S. Embassy in Singapore.

At DEA, INS, and FBI:

DEA

October 4   Firm owning tuna boats causing problems; reported by CIA officer in Singapore.

October 12   Bombing in Bali is reported on all of the news wires and governmental services.

October 21   Odd commercial activity by tuna boat company; reported by Commerce Section at U.S. Embassy in Singapore.

October 24   Possible relationship between intercepted tuna boats and Baltimore–Philadelphia activity; reported by Miami DEA.

November 1   Odd hiring practice at the Singapore harbor, new tuna boat activity, and potential for economic recovery; October 23 report from Economics officer in Singapore.

November 5   The names of five of the tuna boat captains; reported by Maryland Coast Guard.

November 7   Background checks on the five tuna boat captains.

November 8   Commercial, economic, and personal information on the tuna boats and the Seattle news article are possibly correlated; reported by CIA officer in Singapore.

INS

October 12 Bombing in Bali is reported on all of the news wires and governmental services.

October 28 An unusual number of students returning home; reported by Singapore Desk at CIA Headquarters.

November 1 Odd hiring practice at the Singapore harbor, new tuna boat activity, and potential for economic recovery; October 23 report from Economics officer at U.S. Embassy in Singapore.

November 5 The names of five of the tuna boat captains; reported by Maryland Coast Guard.

November 7 Background checks on the five tuna boat captains.

FBI

October 12 Bombing in Bali is reported on all of the news wires and governmental services.

October 16 Panama-flagged boats acting uncooperatively in Baltimore and possible relationship to tuna boat activity at Philadelphia; reported by Maryland Coast Guard.

October 21 Odd commercial activity by tuna boat company; reported by Commerce Section at U.S. Embassy in Singapore.

October 24 Possible relationship between intercepted tuna boats and Baltimore–Philadelphia activity; reported by Miami DEA.

November 1 Odd hiring practice at the Singapore harbor, new tuna boat activity, and potential for economic recovery; October 23 report from Economics officer at U.S. Embassy in Singapore.

November 5 The names of five of the tuna boat captains; from Maryland Coast Guard.

November 7   Background checks on the five tuna boat captains.

The analysis . . .

It is clear in hindsight that there were many clues and signals floating in the system and that much of the information was sitting on the desks. For example, by November 8, the collective knowledge was:

October 4   Since mid-September, owners of 18 tuna boats had been drawing attention to themselves.

October 12   Bombing in Bali was reported on all of the news wires and governmental services.

October 14   On October 13, abandoned luggage was found at the Singapore airport, Saudi Air terminal.

October 14   On September 30, two Arab students were detained for having false driver's licenses at Singapore airport.

October 14   On October 10, a wharf in Philadelphia was leased to a Panamanian firm.

October 14   On October 10, a Panamanian firm requested off-loading privileges in Baltimore.

October 16   Panama-flagged boats acting uncooperatively in Baltimore; possible relationship to tuna boat activity at Philadelphia.

October 16–31   Names of five of the tuna boat captains known.

October 18   Odd commercial activity by tuna boat company.

October 23   Classified ads in Singapore paper for high-paying, cash work on the docks for new Panamanian fishing company.

October 24   Possible relationship between intercepted tuna boats and Baltimore–Philadelphia activity.

October 28	Unusual number of Arab students returning home.
November 4	By August 9, 24 Panamanian tuna boats had arrived in Sydney Harbour.
November 4	Odd commercial activity by tuna boat company.
November 5	On November 1, Seattle reception for Mujen family from Syria.
November 4	Coincidence of tuna boat problems and oddities in Sydney and Singapore.
November 5	Background check on five of the tuna boat captains.
November 8	Commercial, economic, and personal information that the tuna boats and the Seattle news article are possibly correlated.

While other information in the public domain was not caught, there was adequate information in the system—why were the dots not connected in time? Some relationships were picked up by some of the intelligence network, but the big picture eluded everyone. All the agencies and individuals did their job and forwarded information as it was warranted. If everyone did his job, what went wrong? The congressional committee made the following observations:

1. The student forum was not picked up since information flows did not exist with China. Thus, the primary information was unavailable and secondary information traces at the individual level with correlations did not exist. The intelligence system did not pick up the student travel.

2. Delays with the overt and public information resulted in certain information being missed when it could have been helpful. The exporting of ships from Seattle and the harbor information in Sydney were vital.

3. Twenty-four boats were built, but only eighteen were accounted for in Singapore where they were all supposed to be shipped. The

geographic dispersion and secondary companies used to distribute the vessels was not caught. ~~Six boats were unaccounted for.~~

4. Multiple agencies were processing and analyzing related information but were unaware of others doing similar tasks.

5. The information flows were directed by where people thought information should go, not by what people were looking for or where related activities might be.

6. Delays existed for information some sources thought was low-priority when in fact it was significant and high-priority.

7. Analysts within the same agencies were often sitting on the same or related information without being aware of it.

8. It was more by accident than by design that the tuna boat construction in Seattle was linked into the limited picture that government agencies had prior to 11/9. If the Chamber of Commerce had not announced the reception, the link would never have been made.

Application of the ASAP Architecture

A fully functional ASAP system would have a large number of different status-quo agents watching entities, looking for what was out-of-the-ordinary, and setting and testing hypotheses. There would be agents for "interesting" events such as financial transactions, movement of people, and data communication. In this section we will give several examples of possible status-quo agents and explain how such agents would have operated in the above scenario.

First, consider an *import/export agent.* Things imported come from somewhere, leave at a specific time, and have characteristics such as importer, exporter, shipper, owner, weight, volume, and quantities. Things exported are supposed to go somewhere, arrive at some time, and have a number of characteristics as well. A status-quo expectation would be that what is exported in one jurisdiction is imported by another with the various characteristics largely intact. Similarly, if something is imported, there should have been export records, and—if the goods come from a friendly nation—the information should be available. If something is exported to a friendly nation, eventually there should be matching import records. The watching import/export agent would monitor these types of characteristics and note deviations from the expectation. A holistic approach would be used to identify similar or "close enough" matches to catch the cases where certain information is changed en route. If something has been changed, a flag would be raised at the expected arrival time (within a threshold) when the matching import records are not generated for the expected items.

It is reasonable to expect that, given the systems and projects under way today, this type of information should be available for analysis. What would this information have meant in the tuna boat scenario? When the export records were filed for the 24 tuna boats, an entry would have been made to watch for the corresponding life cycle of the transaction. A timer would have been set to catch the nonclosure, and pattern-matching would have been performed on the various characteristics to catch one or more of the attributes being changed en route. The export information would also contain the shipping and sailing manifest and planned ports of call. In due course:

1. The arrival of 24 tuna boats in Australia instead of Singapore would have been noted as possibly unusual and flagged for any secondary processing to pick up relationships.

2. The arrival of 18 boats in Singapore instead of 24 would have been noted. This would have been related to the fact of the different export location, and the information would have been forwarded to various agencies.

3. Assuming some delays in paperwork and associated processing, the destination mismatch should have been noted by mid-August and the quantity mismatch by mid-September. The first report would not likely trigger a great deal of interest, but when significant as-

sets go missing combined with irregularities in transit behavior, a focused analysis by the intelligence community to probe further would likely have been launched.

4. If Sydney had been listed as a planned port of call, the first trap would have been missed, but the change in quantity would have been caught. Transit is a more fluid characteristic and some flexibility exists in that dimension. However, a change in a physical characteristic is of more interest. If the travel itinerary or route change had included hostile or questionable ports of call, this would have been added to the analysis with a corresponding rise in priority or interest.

5. The dot connector algorithm would have correlated the Seattle, Australia, and Singapore information by mid-September and highlighted this coincidence to the appropriate analysts and agencies.

In this scenario, the information would have been brought to the intelligence agencies approximately four to six weeks earlier. Furthermore, the information would have been brought forward without relying on Scott's reading of the Seattle newspaper and the informal intelligence gathering that occurred at the embassy. The import and export information is factual, quantifiable, and can be captured and computerized. Since assets are often moved from point A to point B across national borders with expected behaviors, an import/export analyzer will be an important part of the ASAP detector.

Second, consider a *commerce analyzer*. Not all aspects of commerce are interesting. For example, a new dry cleaner or corner variety store is not normally of note. However, commerce that involves movement of goods in and out of harbors and airfields would be, as would transportation patterns across borders. Commerce that involves modes of transportation and shipment would also be interesting. Because there are expected trends and behaviors of commerce, it is possible to construct commerce watchers. For example, consider the tuna boat story again. When a business requests a license to operate in the transport or goods movement sector, or to operate a processing facility at (or close to) an entry or exit point, the business can undergo a status-quo check. Existing business databases can be checked for the region and patterns analyzed. Possible patterns to review are the following: any existing or similar firms (if none, why a new entrant?), percentage of change in capacity (if a small increment in base, it's probably okay, but a significant increase would be odd), business trend data (if decreasing sector, why a new entrant?), and so forth. Standard codes exist for industry sector, type of business, and so on, and these can be exploited when searching for business patterns. Historical data can be used to identify the patterns for new entrants and the normal size of players in the sector in terms of capacity. These are "expected behaviors" and any significant deviation may be noteworthy. Each noteworthy observation is a dot.

1. In the tuna boat story, we might have caught an unusual increase in tuna boats being built and an odd fleet renewal pattern, or an unusual number of tuna boats operating in Singapore, or the oddity of the existence and operation of tuna boats in the Maryland jurisdiction.

2. There were three possible commerce-oriented dots by mid-October. The *dot connector* agent would have added this information to the other tuna boat information and widened its backsweep and possible relationship searches—owners, operators, ports of call, cargo, and crew.

The result from this agent, which highlighted the commerce dots, might have been the possible connection of the Mujen name and firms somewhat related to unusual activities in different parts of the world at the same time. The Coast Guard and Maryland Port Authority would probably have noted the odd port behavior just as quickly, but this would not have been so easily correlated with the Far East activities without a dot connector.

As a third and last example, consider a *student association watcher* that tracks and watches for status-quo behavior of students on the watch list. In this case, the watcher would pick up the sudden booking of trips and traffic through Singapore. This would be an unusual volume and geographical convergence. The cause—the conference in Hong Kong—would be hidden, and in one sense the dot would be a red herring and would make unwanted noise. There was good reason for the travel and the gathering. However, when the dot was identified, a relationship search was launched for any connections to any other dots or curiosity items. A search would have been done on the membership, attendees, and organizing committee. This might have highlighted the Mujen connection as a possible dot connection and brought it to an analyst's attention for further consideration. This possible relationship would have come to light in mid-October when the travel booking started.

The above three example detector agents are reasonable and feasible to create for asymmetric threats. Agents like these could be created for attributes and characteristics that are considered relevant and that have life cycles and expected behaviors or values. The focus would need to be at the detailed and aggregate levels—for instance, foreign registration versus a specific Panamanian company name. A human could conceivably have seen and recognized the information picked up by the ASAP detector agents. In hindsight, the dots are obvious and should have been connected before 11/9.

The detectors will not catch everything, and they will identify relationships that are red herrings. But over time, the detectors could grow in sophistication as analysts add more rules and items to watch for. Initially, the detectors would be rather coarse and would be limited to picking up changes in status, convergence of assets, continuity failures, and so forth. There are two critical conditions for the ASAP detector—access and availability of data and expectation models. The above example detectors illustrate the type of information that is or should be available and the types of expectations that can be represented in software systems. The expectations and information must be quantitative and cannot be vague or ambiguous — such as "too many" or "too often." The expectations must be based on historical or expected values with normal variability noted.

The Hybrid Element—People in the ASAP Architecture

We have described how several simple information detectors might have operated under the ASAP framework and how this might have affected the tuna boat scenario. However, that is only part of the solution and operational profile. The system does not exist in a vacuum, and it cannot exist outside the current operational fabric of intelligence processing. Human beings are also involved, and they bring strengths and weaknesses to the situation, creating a hybrid structure. Any computer system will undoubtedly raise false signals and miss some obvious ones. Those weaknesses can never be eliminated, but they can be minimized.

The filters described as part of the framework will assist with reducing some of the noise, but noise will certainly exist. In the final analysis, the human element will be critical for deciding what is a dot and whether the dot connection is worthy of further effort. If something is noted by a human as being noise, it will still be kept on file and used for secondary analysis purposes, but unless something else happens that strengthens the signal or the relationship, the noise will be kept in the background. This type of logic helps with the problem of the human dismissing something as noise when it is not. The system will keep an eye on it, just in case. The human can also create specific noise filters to identify and block certain types of known deception and other sources of background noise. This can be done for time windows, targets, or detected dots matching certain criteria. (These filters would be subject to periodic review, to ensure that meaningful data are not being removed accidentally.)

Along with the information (dots and relationships) rising to the top, the analyst will be integrating other information from system databases and from personal knowledge about the situation. Perhaps a dot is a bit "off," but it tweaks something in the analyst's recent memory and the analyst can issue a further ASAP or data mining directive. Perhaps the analyst sees an interesting piece of data otherwise buried and proceeds to call a colleague at another agency. Whatever analysts do will be driven by what they see, what they know, their training, and their personalities. People will vet and judge information based on assumptions and hypotheses about the sources and other disparate data. For example, what is not said might be amplified by the analyst, or what is seen might be discounted or attenuated. This is part of the process. Consider the personalities involved with the tuna vignette:

- Harold R. Tynes: U.S. Ambassador to Singapore. Career Foreign Service officer with a disdain for the intelligence business. Subscribes to the 1940s belief "Gentlemen don't read other gentlemen's mail."

- Mark L. Lupin: CIA Chief of Station, Singapore. Ambitious Directorate of Operations (DO) officer, finally landed a big assignment. Has little time for "coordination." Hot shot with his eyes on bigger fish.

- Randy G. May: CIA "general purpose" case officer, Singapore. Can't seem to get promoted beyond GS-12 and not an overachiever by any means, but somehow gets the job done—eventually.

- Karen P. Scott: State Dept. Commercial Attaché, Singapore. Wanted to see the world after Wharton, so Daddy got her this "broadening" experience. Undergraduate work in fine arts and French. Has a budding romance with the local Singaporean Director of Fine Arts.

- Timothy M. Smythe: Australian liaison partner for Tynes/Lupin. Finds intelligence a rotten business, but hates those "dirty bastards" and is willing to roll up his sleeves. Has been known to bend the rules a bit too; but only Lupin knows this.

- Fred "Woody" Johnson: Singapore Desk Analyst at the CIA's Directorate of Intelligence (DI). Serious regional specialist who thinks he's tuned into the new world order, but longs for "traditional" threats and analyses and the chance to draft a multiyear National Intelligence Estimate.

- Michael Scott "Mack" McDermott: Coast Guard Officer in charge of Border Security for Port of Baltimore. Has just learned he is being transferred to the new Department of Homeland Security (DHS) and is ready to "kick some butt."

- Kevin N. Moore: Deputy Director for Asymmetric Threats, CIA Counter Terrorism Center (CTC). Moore has a 20-year operations background and came into this post soon after 9/11. Moore believes the CTC can make a difference but has never managed an organization with 500+ people from so many diverse government organizations. Paperwork frustrates him as do "meetings for the sake of meetings." He is known to walk out of them if he doesn't feel they are productive.

- Susan B. Mandetti: CIA representative to DEA. Susan, a counterterrorism graduate and GS-14 from the DI, has been offered several rotational assignments and jumped at the chance to mix it up with the tough boys in Florida and see how it's really done. She's enthusiastic, supportive, and goes beyond the call of duty in representing CIA with DEA; really trying to give them the analytical perspective. The problem is, the DEA guys aren't as enthusiastic about Susan as she is about them.

- Sam R. Trowl: Immigration and Naturalization Service (INS) bureaucrat. Been there 29 years, can't wait to retire, but must first survive the transfer to DHS. He's over his head but puts on a good front and tries to help.

- In the background, Trowl's protégé, William D. Sands, is an eager, up-and-coming kid with a bright future who can't seem to do it "the way we've always done it." Seems he's more interested in creativity than conventionality. A bit of a geek.

- Francis Xavier Arden ("Big Frank"): Tough FBI chief of counterintelligence for the Mid-Atlantic region based in Philadelphia. He don't want no spies, thugs, or "rag head" terrorists on his turf. Has embraced the new DHS and recently participated in several CIA, FBI, NSA "counterterrorism coordination" off-site meetings. His little brother was gravely wounded early in the war in Afghanistan.

- Roger T. Anderson: Career SIGINT officer from NSA with overseas field experience as an Arabic linguist. Recently assigned as operations "referent" to ARDA to support their development of technology to help analysts find the needle in the haystack and identify potential terrorist activity.

These individuals can be considered to be example stereotypes of people involved in the intelligence process. There are many more possible personality-driven profiles, and in any situation, none, some, or many of these types of people can be observed. Each brings strengths and weaknesses to the table. For example, some of the individuals would never use or trust a computerized detection mechanism or take the time to create filters or sniffers. Some will delay information while gaining greater confidence while others may pull the trigger too quickly and transmit information full of noise and misleading innuendos. However, some will be proactive and willingly participate in electronic chat rooms, actively set filters, and look at the hit lists created by the tool. People comfortable with online sharing of ideas and thoughts will most likely embrace a tool that enables and facilitates their discussions with trusted colleagues—bouncing ideas, suspicions, and the like.

The ASAP architecture would give the latter types of analysts a tool that complements the basic nature of analysis—thinking about what makes sense (building models of the status quo), watching for anomalies in the situation (the detectors), and drawing hypotheses about anything that draws their attention (the relationship engines). The ASAP tool will not replace these key activities of the human analyst. However, it will be able to watch more data, process it more quickly, and look for possible relationships within the data universe.

Systems Related to the ASAP Architecture

Systems Complementary to the ASAP Architecture

ASAP systems will fit into existing and future intelligence analysis and production "supply chains" well. Below, we describe several major intelligence support systems, both extant and under development, that would provide strong, complementary environments that ASAP could leverage (and that in turn could leverage ASAP).

A key feature of ASAP is that it is a hybrid system, dividing analysis labor between humans and automated agents. The idea of a division of labor between man and machine to support intelligence analysis is not new in intelligence analysis. For example, machine (assisted) translation tools are inadequate to produce final products but are good enough to do that "first cut," leaving enough good material for an analyst to work with or enough to be sent to a human, professional translator for final editing. Similarly, the CIA Counter-Terrorism Center's (CTC's) DEFT[1] (Data Extraction From Text) worked in a manner complementary to analysts both by looking for patterns, such as known terrorists, weapons, aliases, and transactions, and by automatically populating the CTC's (and therefore the intelligence community's) Counter Terrorism Database. However, the system was never on "autopilot." Once DEFT had done what it could

---

[1] DEFT was the first artificial intelligence system deployed to an intelligence production environment. One of the authors of this monograph (Snyder) conceived, designed, and managed the system in 1988 while working at the CIA.

do first—plough through megabytes and megabytes (this was the 1980s) of unformatted text and populate more than 90 percent of the database, the analysts did what they did best—resolved ambiguity and exercised human judgment and intuition before the final elements were frozen in the database. This may sound like a technical exercise, but bear in mind that it was designed based on how analysts worked at the time: looking for known patterns; looking for "more of the same." Many programs and tools, such as DARPA's TIPSTER program,[2] have given analysts the horsepower to find the relevant documents and query large collections of data for information they felt they needed. ASAP systems will leverage these search-and-query tools to help locate data for further analysis.

The intelligence community now has a number of systems that identify incoming data, mainly textual, including transcripts of communications, reports from imagery analysts, and intelligence from other sources, and triage the data into the right domain "bin." Once binned, analysts "mine" the bins and use pattern-matching or pattern-generating tools based on their own strategies and tactics. Consistent with the literature, analysts lay out multiple sets of data as various patterns or pictures emerge. They are not building a collection of piece-parts to yield one grand mosaic (as is commonly described); rather, they are leveraging broad datasets to "see" various pictures take shape (see Heuer, 1999[3]). The niche we see ASAP filling

---

[2] Described at http://www.itl.nist.gov/iad/894.02/related_projects/tipster/overv.htm.

[3] Heuer strongly criticizes the common "mosaic" perspective of analysis in the *Psychology of Intelligence Analysis*:

> Understanding of the analytic process has been distorted by the mosaic metaphor commonly used to describe it. According to the mosaic theory of intelligence, small pieces of information are collected that, when put together like a mosaic or jigsaw puzzle, eventually enable analysts to perceive a clear picture of reality. The analogy suggests that accurate estimates depend primarily upon having all the pieces—that is, upon accurate and relatively complete information. It is important to collect and store the small pieces of information, as these are the raw material from which the picture is made; one never knows when it will be possible for an astute analyst to fit a piece into the puzzle. Part of the rationale for large technical intelligence collection system is rooted in this mosaic theory.
>
> Insights from cognitive psychology suggest that intelligence analysts do not work this way and that the most difficult analytical tasks cannot be approached in this manner. Analysts commonly find pieces that appear to fit many different pictures. Instead of a

is providing the pieces that are related to a picture (established pattern) but that do not fit into it nicely. There has to be some reason why a piece of the story that used to make so much sense now "just doesn't add up." Since the piece doesn't fit the story anymore (that is, it deviates from the established pattern), ASAP will put it, along with related data and possible explanations, in front of the analyst to consider.

Beginning with the fundamental data, the FBI's Gateway Information Sharing Initiative (GISI) can search the full text of investigative records, use natural language-processing algorithms to identify key elements within those records (names, addresses, phone numbers, etc.), and graphically depict relationships between these elements. Such basic information elements as addresses and phone numbers and other raw data generated by text recognition would feed into ASAP. We see GISI as one of the primary systems accessed by the ASAP architecture's interceptor agents. In addition to linked law enforcement records, GISI would provide ASAP systems with other basic elements, such as chronologies, analytical reviews, time lines, charts, and graphs, as well as access to myriad law enforcement and commercial databases. Legal and policy issues would need to be reviewed before a primarily foreign intelligence system would be allowed to share countless law enforcement and domestic databases.

In addition to collecting observational data, ASAP would also need to collect data on what analysts are doing and what their reports contain. The Novel Intelligence from Massive Data (NIMD)[4] pro-

---

picture emerging from putting all the pieces together, analysts typically form a picture first and then select the pieces to fit. Accurate estimates depend at least as much upon the mental model used in forming the picture as upon the number of pieces of the puzzle that have been collected. (Heuer, 1999, pp. 61–62)

[4] Described at http://www.ic-arda.org/Novel_Intelligence/. NIMD describes one of its own value-added functions as follows: "We believe that novel intelligence is likely to result from recognizing the assumptions, biases, and hypotheses that drive an analysis and systematically helping analysts challenge or extend them. For example, if a key assumption is negated, then it is reasonable that a different outcome might be expected—potentially a strategic surprise. Ultimately, we believe that the most powerful analytic environment will be one in which information about analysts is not only induced from their activities (as captured through NIMD's Glass Box Analyst), but in which they also have an active hand in explicitly constructing and manipulating representations or models of the analytic targets that contain and

gram would provide ASAP access to analysts' models and behavior in unique ways. NIMD is aimed at focusing analytic attention on the most critical information found within massive amounts of data—information that indicates the potential for strategic surprise. We see two key aspects of NIMD that would complement ASAP.

First, NIMD claims to be developing tools and techniques that capture the synergy forged and developed between analysts and information, so that intelligence analysis may

- be guided by analysts' evolving mental creations, understanding, and knowledge throughout a tightly coupled interactive and spiraling process whose virtual result may be likened to an effective devil's advocate
- reveal new indicators, issues, and/or threats that would not otherwise have been found because of the great mass of data.

The output of NIMD here would help keep ASAP's agents updated with respect to the types of data that NIMD-assisted analysts are finding to be worth further analysis—especially those types that did not fit into previous patterns and mindsets. Similarly, NIMD outputs would update ASAP hypothesis agents when particular assumptions or expectations are found to have been invalidated.

Second, using NIMD's Glass Box Analyst environment, ASAP would be able to "look over an analyst's shoulder" as the analyst both interacts with the data and personally tweaks the models and assumptions that the system uses. The resulting behavioral data would directly feed ASAP agents that work on analyst-related information.

Work at DARPA, in particular the Evidence Extraction and Link Discovery Program (EELD),[5] currently managed by Ted Senator, also complements ASAP's functionality and goals. Although both systems incorporate context, ASAP works with dynamic contex-

---

make explicit their knowledge, interests, hypotheses and biases, and other traits of their analytic state."

[5] Described in a DARPA Tech 2000 presentation given by Senator, available at http://www.darpa.mil/DARPATech2002/presentations/iao_pdf/speeches/SENATOR.pdf.

tual rules, whereas EELD works with the individual elements of context in the data and information sense. In particular, EELD scans large amounts of data (usually gleaned from text) to derive "factual relationships" between different entities (EELD is similar to GISI and the ASAP architecture's first-order relationship agents in this respect). The factual relationships are filed in a large "evidence database," and the contents of the database becomes the "context." Then, as new data are scanned by the system, EELD attempts to link the new data to existing facts and analyzes the resulting structures of links to determine whether they match patterns representing potentially unusual behavior. EELD will also attempt to use new learning methodologies to recognize previously unknown patterns of interest. Senator describes EELD's use of context as follows:

> Activities such as getting a pilot's license, or purchasing airline tickets with cash at the last minute, or overstaying a visa, are not by themselves indicators of terrorist behavior. In fact, the most dangerous adversaries will be the ones who most successfully disguise their individual transactions to appear normal, reasonable, and legitimate. It is only when they are combined in a particular way, or, in other words, they occur in a particular context, that they become highly unusual.[6]

We envision information exchanges between ASAP and EELD running in both directions. Linked datasets discovered by EELD and matching ASAP interceptor criteria or ASAP relationship agents' queries can be used as inputs to ASAP's dot-finding, linking, and hypothesis-generating agents. Conversely, ASAP's pattern templates (agents for data interception, hypothesis generating, and hypothesis testing) can be used to create and dynamically update pattern-testing agents within EELD.

---

[6] Quote from Senator's DARPA Tech 2002 presentation, available at http://www.darpa.mil/DARPATech2002/presentations/iao_pdf/speeches/SENATOR.pdf.

Systems and Analytic Tools That Might Help Implement the Framework

A number of government and commercial off-the-shelf systems have components that might be used to implement parts of a real-world ASAP system. In this section, we consider existing technologies and systems that might be used as infrastructure and architecture components, analysis agents, and/or tools to assist analysts.

Architecture and Infrastructure Platforms

The ASAP architecture depends on the successful interaction and control of a large number of distributed agents and data storage nodes. A natural software platform for implementing ASAP systems could be the Cognitive Agent Architecture (COUGAAR), a DARPA-developed open-source architecture for large-scale multiagent systems. It is based on a cognitive model of human thinking and interaction, which "attempts to emulate the mental processes of perception, memory, judgment, reasoning and decision making. The architecture utilizes a hybrid task and data representation of cognition to represent complex, dynamic plans. This architecture also supports fine-grained information management, dynamic task allocation, data fusion, and execution based replanning and assessment."[7]

Similarly, Intelliseek is creating an open architecture, based on extensible markup language (XML) transactions, which allows the integration of disjoint information search and analysis tools into the same overall system.[8] This architecture might allow the incorporation of existing software products into ASAP without requiring significant recoding of the software products.

---

[7] COUGAAR's home page, which provides summary documentation, full technical references, and development software, is http://www.cougaar.org. The quote is from project contractor BBN's web page on COUGAAR, http://www.bbn.com/abs/caa.html.

[8] Described in the March 2003 *Technology Review* article "Can Sensemaking Keep Us Safe?" (Waldrop, 2003).

Implementations of ASAP Agents

A number of organizations are working on tools that might become components of some of the agents in the ASAP architecture. First, IBM is developing technologies supporting the creation of "federated" information systems. A federated information system consists of multiple, disjoint databases in which each database has a "wrapper" that converts a standard query language into commands for that particular database. The wrapper also converts the database's response into standard formats. In addition, the wrapper can be used to set security and privacy restrictions—providing statistical measures without providing actual records, for example. Such "wrapper" objects might be used for the parts of ASAP interceptor agents that physically work with external databases.[9]

Systems Research and Development's NORA (Non-Obvious Relationship Awareness) software shows promise for implementing portions of the interceptor and first-order relationship agents. Part of the NORA software takes incoming data from various data feeds and converts it into XML in a common format, which is one of the important tasks of an interceptor agent. Another part of the NORA software attempts to link the incoming records with other records currently in the NORA database. The NORA software employs fuzzy logic algorithms to detect links obscured by data errors or intentional deception. For example, suppose Alice attempts and is denied a U.S. entry visa but decides to apply for another one using a different identity, in which the new identity has reversed digits for the birth date and the same U.S. phone number and address; NORA would identify the two visa applications as both being for Alice. In one implementation, NORA software addresses nine million transactions per day coming from over four thousand data feeds.[10]

In an ASAP system, NORA might be augmented by Attensity's Early Warning and Response (EWR) system. EWR scans free-form

---

[9] Described in Waldrop (2003). For technical information, see Jhingran, Mattos, and Pirahesh (2002) and Roth et al. (2002).

[10] NORA's home page, which provides briefings describing the system, is http://www.srdnet.com/prod_nora.html.

text documents to extract pieces of information, then puts the information into "normalized, analysis-ready, tabular data." For example, an EWR system applied to a company's customer comments and repair forms would identify the parts causing the most problems and the most frequently stated reasons for customer dissatisfaction. In ASAP, EWR might be used for interceptor agents that want to extract data objects from free-form text files.[11]

Stratify's Discovery System shows potential for implementing other portions of the dot-finding and first-order relationship agents. The Discovery System scans textual documents and extracts their underlying concepts (similar to EWR), then sorts the documents using a taxonomy of concepts and groups the documents into clusters by conceptual similarity. The taxonomy used can either be an external input or can be generated automatically from the Discovery System's analysis of the documents. This system might be valuable in detecting text file dots based on their content, as well as finding first-order links between text files. The system might even have some use in implementing second-order agents in terms of tracking whether there are surges in the numbers of documents containing particular records.[12]

Mohomine's MohoClassifier also scans text files to place them into categories within a taxonomy and is worthy of evaluation for use within an ASAP system. This system does not use concepts, however; it uses pattern recognition algorithms to place text files within categories given sets of documents provided to the system as exemplars of the categories. Like Stratify's Discovery System, this system might also have use in detecting text file dots based on their content.[13]

---

[11] Attensity's home page is http://www.attensity.com. EWR is also described on the In-Q-Tel home page, http://www.in-q-tel.com. In-Q-Tel is a private, nonprofit venture capital agency funded and managed by the Central Intelligence Agency.

[12] Stratify's home page is http://www.stratify.com; also described in Waldrop (2003).

[13] Mohomine's home page is http://www.mohomine.com; it is also described on the In-Q-Tel home page, http://www.in-q-tel.com. Note that Mohomine is developing a product for extracting pieces of information from free-form text files that can then be placed in a database, similar to Attensity and Stratify. One of Mohomine's primary applications of this product is to convert resumes into a set of standard employment fields.

Recall that the ASAP architecture includes agents that examine what analysts are doing and what their outputs are in addition to agents that examine observational data. Tacit Knowledge System's Activenet might provide an important base for such agents. Activenet maintains a database of profiles on people within an organization and provides a list of key topics for each individual pertaining to his or her work. The profiles are updated dynamically as people work on new projects or put out reports in particular areas. Employees can then search the database to find people whose work relates to their current projects and initiate communications with those people. (The specific results that any employee is allowed to see are restricted by a security system.) Such a system might be very useful in searching for analysts who are looking at particular types of information or who are putting out reports on particular topics.[14]

Implementation of Tools to Assist Analysts

An important issue in creating an effective machine-human analyst relationship in ASAP is to provide human-understandable justifications for the datasets found to be "worth further analysis." Several tools provide such justifications; the first of these is the EELD subsidiary program AHEAD (Analogical Hypothesis Elaborator for Activity Detection—see Murdock, Aha, and Breslow, 2002). When a dataset is found to meet criteria that make it worth further investigation (in the case of AHEAD, the criterion is matching a pattern indicating a possible asymmetric threat), AHEAD generates a human-readable report giving a list of reasons why the dataset is worth further investigation, as well as a list of reasons why the dataset might simply be noise. This tool could be directly employed as part of the hypothesis-generating and -reporting functionalities of ASAP.

Analyst's Notebook, by the Cambridge, England, company i2, is a set of data visualization tools that graphically show the links between entities (the software provides time lines, geographic maps, and transaction analysis charts for displaying the links). Each link in the

---

[14] Tacit Knowledge Systems is described on the In-Q-Tel home page, http://www.in-q-tel.com. The company's home page, which features Activenet, is http://www.tacit.com.

chart connects to the evidence for that link (the specific data objects implying the link). All charts are dynamically updatable; a new data object or a data object found to be false generates or deletes links accordingly.[15]

MetaCarta's Geographic Text Search Appliance is a combination search-and-visualization tool that associates documents with geographic locations. The tool allows analysts to search for documents by specific location and to display sets of documents related to particular locations on a map. The company maintains a large, regularly updated database of maps and geographic locations to support the search-and-display features.[16]

SRI International's Structured Evidential Argumentation System (SEAS), part of DARPA's Project Genoa, structures evidence for and against a particular hypothesis by creating trees of yes-no questions in which the likely answer to a question depends on the answer to lower-level questions. The resulting tree guides analysts in getting from low-level observational data (the evidence) to a logical guess of whether or not a particular hypothesis is true (the root question in the tree).[17] Similar in character to SEAS are the SAIC products Situational Influence Assessment Model tool (SIAM) and Causeway, both of which support the creation of influence networks that describe how events and analysts' beliefs eventually lead to an educated guess of the validity of a hypothesis.[18]

---

[15] i2's home page is http://www.i2.co.uk; Analysts' Notebook is also described in Waldrop (2003). Note that i2 makes a database called iBase that is specifically designed to work with Analyst's Notebook and other visualization tools and a program called iBridge that allows Analyst's Notebook to access data in other databases.

[16] MetaCarta's home page is http://www.metacarta.com; also described on In-Q-Tel's home page, http://www.in-q-tel.com.

[17] SEAS's home page is http://www.ai.sri.com/~seas/, also described in Waldrop (2003). Project Genoa's home page is http://www.darpa.mil/iao/Genoa.htm (accessed April 2003).

[18] The home page for SIAM and Causeway is http://www.inet.saic.com/welcome_ to_saic.htm; Rosen and Smith (2000) provide an introduction to the software and its applications. These products employ Bayesian influence networks to calculate numerical estimates that a given hypothesis is true given estimates for other, influencing hypotheses; Rosen and Smith (1996) describe the technique.

From the above list, it is clear that many possible existing and emerging systems might be useful within an ASAP system. Furthermore, over time some of the systems will evolve, possibly become extinct, and be replaced with the next generation of analysis tool. ASAP must be built with these characteristics in mind and should resemble a carpenter's tool with interchangeable accessories. Toward that end, a virtual machine architecture[19] would be designed for ASAP agents and the data flows within and between ASAP components. The virtual machine layer would normalize the internal data flows using object-oriented techniques and would allow data definitions and functionality to be extended and changed over time. Normalization filters would be the integration components for the various pieces of technology used for specific tasks. A data flow and analysis system that is based on the concepts of problem solving would be developed, with a language containing such concepts as suspicions, primary evidence, supporting evidence, and hypotheses. Such a system would allow various components to be swapped in and out of use without destabilizing the operational base. Similar approaches to isolating system dependencies (e.g., IBM's CP/67, VM/370) have been successfully used in computer operating systems since the early 1970s.

---

[19] We use the classic IBM definition for *virtual machine architecture* (compare TechTarget's Whatis.com IT encyclopedia, http://www.whatis.com). In this definition, a virtual machine architecture supports multiple software applications simultaneously. It brokers shared network resources between the applications and provides inter-application communications while giving each application the impression that it is running on an individual computer and has sole control of that computer's resources.

Bibliography

Advanced Research and Development Activity (ARDA). 2002. "Novel Intelligence from Massive Data." Available at http://www.ic-arda.org/Novel_Intelligence/index.html.

Attensity Corporation. 2002. "Attensity Corporation." Available at http://www.attensity.com.

BBN Technologies. 2002. "What We Do: Agent-Based Systems: Cognitive Agent Architecture." Available at http://www.bbn.com/abs/caa.html.

Braun, Stephen, and Mark Fineman. 2002. "Sniper Suspects Slipped Past Authorities Time and Again." *Los Angeles Times*, November 30, p. A1.

Cabena, Peter, et al. (IBM International Technical Support Organization). 1998. *Discovering Data Mining: From Concept to Implementation*. Upper Saddle River, NJ: Prentice Hall PTR.

Carbonell, Jaime, ed. 1990. *Machine Learning: Paradigms and Methods*. Cambridge: MIT Press.

Cloudmakers. "Cloudmakers.org," 2002. Available at http://www.cloudmakers.org.

Congressional Joint Inquiry into September 11th. 2002. *Final Report of the Congressional Joint Inquiry into September 11th*. December 11.

Cougaar Group. 2002. "Cougaar Home Page." Available at http://www.cougaar.org, accessed May 2002.

DARPA Information Awareness Office. 2003a. "Evidence Extraction and Link Discovery (EELD)." http://www.darpa.mil/iao/EELD.htm, acessed April 2003.

_____. 2002. "Genoa." http://www.darpa.mil/iao/Genoa.htm, accessed April 2003.

_____. 2003b. "Genoa II." http://www.darpa.mil/iao/GenoaII.htm, ac-
cessed April 2003.

_____. "Terrorism Information Awareness (TIA) System," 2003c.
http://www.darpa.mil/iao/TIASystems.htm, accessed April 2003.

_____. "Wargaming the Asymmetric Environment (WAE)," 2003d.
http://www.darpa.mil/iao/WAE.html, accessed April 2003.

Delugach, Harry. 2003. "Conceptual Graphs Home Page," Available at
http://www.cs.uah.edu/~delugach/CG/, accessed April 2003.

Department of Justice. 2002. "Attorney General John Ashcroft Unveils
Gateway Information Sharing Pilot Project in St. Louis, Missouri." Department of Justice Press Release AG 02-589, October 9, 2002. Available
at http:// www.usdoj.gov/opa/pr/2002/October/02_ag_589.htm.

Diamond, John. 2002. "Terror Group's Messengers Steer Clear of NSA
Ears." *USA Today*, October 18, p. A12.

Dulles, Allen. 1963. *The Craft of Intelligence*. New York: Harper & Row.

Eggen, Dan, and Glenn Kessler. 2002. "Signs of Terror Said to Increase;
Officials Say Tape, 'Chatter' Indicate Plans for Attacks." *Washington
Post*, Nov 14, p. A1.

Elliot, Michael. 2002. "How Al-Qaeda Got Back on the Attack." *Time*,
October 20.

Goering, Laurie. 2002. "I Shook Hands With Fire: Kenyan Farmer Talked
to Bomber Minutes Before They Blew Up Hotel." *Chicago Tribune*, December 2, p. 1.

Google. 2003. "Google Technology." Available at http://www.google.com/
technology/.

Heuer, Richard J. 1999. *Psychology of Intelligence Analysis*, CIA Center for
the Study of Intelligence. Available at http://www.cia.gov/csi/books/
19104/index.html.

Hollywood, John S., and Kenneth N. McKay. Forthcoming. *Supplying Information: Managing Information Networks to Meet User and Mission
Needs*. Santa Monica, CA: RAND Corporation, MR-1756-NSA.

i2 Ltd. 2002. "i2 Investigative Analysis Software." Available at http:// www.
i2.co.uk,

In-Q-Tel. 2002. "In-Q-Tel. " Available at http://www.in-q-tel.com.

Intelligence Community Advanced Research and Development Activity.
2002. "Novel Intelligence from Massive Data." Available at
http://www.icarda.org/Novel_Intelligence/.

Jhingran, A. D., N. Mattos, and H. Pirahesh. 2002. "Information Integration: A Research Agenda." *IBM Systems Journal*, Vol. 41, No. 4. Available at http://www.research.ibm.com/journal/sj41-4.html.

Jones, R. V., 1978. *Most Secret War*. London: Hamish Hamilton.

Manjoo, Farhad, 2001. "AI: Unraveling the Mysteries." *Wired News*, June 28.

McKay, K. N. 1992. "Production Planning and Scheduling: A Model for Manufacturing Decisions Requiring Judgement." Ph.D. dissertation, Department of Management Sciences, University of Waterloo, Ontario.

McKay, K. N., J. A. Buzacott, N. Charness, and F. R. Safayeni. 1992. "The Scheduler's Predictive Expertise: An Interdisciplinary Perspective," in G. I. Doukidis and R. J. Paul (eds.), *Artificial Intelligence in Operational Research—Journal of the Operational Research Society*, London: Macmillan Press, pp. 139–150.

McKay K. N., F. R. Safayeni, and J. A. Buzacott. 1995a. "Schedulers & Planners: What and How Can We Learn From Them?" In D. E. Brown and W. T. Scherer (eds.), *Intelligent Scheduling Systems*, Boston: Kluwer Publishers, pp. 41–62.

_____. 1995b. "Common Sense Realities in Planning and Scheduling Printed Circuit Board Production." *International Journal of Production Research*, Vol. 33, No. 6, pp. 1587–1603.

McKay, K. N., and V.C.S. Wiers. 2003. "Planning, Scheduling and Dispatching Tasks in Production Control." *International Journal on Cognition, Technology and Work*, Vol. 5, No. 2, June, pp. 82–93.

Meserve, Jeanne, et al. 2002. "Two Arrested in Sniper Case." CNN.com, October 24.

MetaCarta, Inc. 2003. "MetaCarta: The Geographic Text Search Company." Available at http://www.metacarta.com,

Mohomine, Inc. 2002. "Mohomine: Making Computers Understand People." Available at http://www.mohomine.com.

Murdock, William J., David W. Aha, and Leonard A. Breslow. 2002. "AHEAD: Case-Based Process Model Explanation of Asymmetric Threats." Navy Center for Applied Research in Artificial Intelligence Technical Note AIC-02-203. Available at http://www.aic.nrl.navy.mil/~aha/papers/AIC-02-203.pdf, accessed October 2002.

National Institute of Standards and Technology Information Access Division. 2001. "TIPSTER Text Program." Available at http://www.

itl.nist.gov/iad/894.02/related_projects/tipster/overv.htm, accessed January 2001.

Neustadt, Richard E., and Ernest R. May. 1988. *Thinking in Time: The Uses of History for Decision Makers*. New York: Free Press.

"One Year On: The Hunt for al-Qaida." 2002. *The Guardian*, September 5, p. 6.

PC AI Magazine. 2002. "PC AI—Blackboard Technology." Available at http://www.pcai.com/web/ai_info/blackboard_technology.html.

Rich, Elaine. 1983. *Artificial Intelligence*. New York: McGraw-Hill.

Risen, James. 2003. "US Increased Alert on Evidence Qaeda was Planning Two Attacks." *New York Times*, February 14.

Rolington, Alfred. 2002. "9/11: In Search of Context and Meaning." *Jane's International Security News*, September 11.

Rosen, Julie A., and Wayne L. Smith. 1996. "Influence Net Modeling with Causal Strengths: An Evolutionary Approach." *Proceedings of Command and Control Research and Technology*. Available at http://www.inet.saic.com/, accessed April 2003.

———, 2000. "Influence Net Modeling for Strategic Planning: A Structured Approach to Information Operations." *Phalanx*, Vol. 33, No. 4. Available at http://www.inet.saic.com/. Accessed April 2003.

Roth, M. A., D. C. Wolfson, J. C. Kleewein, and C. J. Nelin. 2002. "Information Integration: A New Generation of Information Technology." *IBM Systems Journal*, Vol. 41, No. 4. Available at http://www.research.ibm.com/journal/sj41-4.html.

Sieberg, Daniel. 2001. "Reality Blurs, Hype Builds with Web 'A.I.' Game." CNN.com, June 13.

Science Applications International Corporation. 2002. "Welcome to SAIC's Influence Net Web Site." Available at http://www.inet.saic.com/welcome_to_saic.htm.

Senator, Ted. 2002. "Evidence Extraction and Link Discovery Program." Presentation at DARPATech 2002 Symposium, August 2. Available at http://www.darpa.mil/DARPATech2002/presentations/iao_pdf/speeches/SENATOR.pdf.

Soltis, Andy. 2003. "WTC Vid Declares Planning of Attack." *New York Post*, March 4.

Sowa, John F. 1974. "Conceptual Graphs for a Database Interface," *IBM Journal of Research and Development*. Volume 20, No. 4, pp. 336–357.

Sowa, John F. 2000. *Knowledge Representation: Logical, Philosophical, and Computational Foundations.* Pacific Grove, CA: Brooks Cole Publishing Co.

SRI International. 2000. "SEAS: A Corporate Memory of Analytic Products and Methods." Available at http://www.ai.sri.com/~seas/.

Stratify, Inc. 2003. "Stratify—Discover More." Available at http://www.stratify.com/.

Systems Research and Development. 2002. "NORA: Non-Obvious Relationship Awareness." Available at http://www.srdnet.com/nora.htm.

Tacit Knowledge Systems, Inc. 2002. "Tacit: Enterprise Collaboration Management." Available at http://www.tacit.com.

TechTarget. 2003. "WhatIs.com." Available at http://www.whatis.com.

"Videotape Shows Preparation for US Attacks—ABC." 2003. Reuters, March 4.

Waldrop, Mitchell. 2003. "Can Sensemaking Keep Us Safe?" *Technology Review.* Available at http://www.technologyreview.com/articles/waldrop0303.asp.

Winer, David. 2002. "The History of Weblogs." Available at http://newhome.weblogs.com/historyOfWeblogs. Accessed May 2002.